Hiking in Grizzly Country

Lessons Learned and Shared

Tim Rubbert

Hiking in Grizzly Country: Lessons Learned and Shared

Published by Riverbend Publishing, Helena, Montana

ISBN: 978-1-60639-115-0

Printed in USA

1 2 3 4 5 6 7 8 FN 26 25 24 23 22

Cover and text design by Sarah Cauble, sarahcauble.com

Riverbend Publishing
P.O. Box 5833
Helena, MT 59604
riverbendpublishing.com

DEDICATION

To John and Frank Craighead whose books and studies gave me invaluable insights into grizzlies, their habitat, and the importance of the conservation and protection of these magnificent animals. To Chuck Jonkle and Andy Russell, both of whom I had the pleasure of spending time in the field, and their different, but valuable observations and experiences which led to my greater understanding of the great bear. And last, but not least, to Brian Peck who fought the good fight and tirelessly advocated for the preservation of the grizzly, its habitat, and other wildlife.

ALSO BY TIM RUBBERT

Hiking With Grizzlies: Lessons Learned

Hiking Safely in Grizzly Country: More Lessons Learned

CONTENTS

INTRODUCTION

The sighting of my first grizzly literally changed my life. It was on a beautiful morning in Yellowstone National Park on Friday, May 24, 1985. I was driving up a winding road towards a high mountain pass when I saw a person in a pullout looking through a video camera with a large telephoto lens towards a far-off mountain shoulder. I turned off into the rather small pullout. I got out and eagerly approached the camera person and asked, wishfully, what he saw. He stated rather excitedly that he was videoing a mating pair of grizzlies. My jaw dropped. I immediately returned to my car and retrieved my film camera with my telephoto lens and tripod (I was prepared for an event such as this). I then set up next to my "new friend" as he pointed out the two amorous bears. I couldn't believe it! I started taking pictures even though the bears were about a mile away. I didn't care; they were the first grizzlies I ever saw.

I soon learned that the spot I was looking at was called "Honeymoon Ridge." Obviously, it was aptly named. I could not believe my good fortune. My first sighting was not just one grizzly, but two: a mating pair! Since I moved to Montana in 1983, I had been reading books on grizzlies to learn about this elusive and "mysterious" creature. I had been looking to spot one whenever I was in Glacier or Yellowstone or along the Rocky Mountain Front. I had not been successful. I really didn't know what I was doing. With no other resources, it was difficult to figure out where to look. Since that first sighting, events changed drastically.

I read every book on grizzlies I could get my hands on. I went to Interagency Grizzly Bear Committee (IGBC) meetings, and every workshop, seminar, and grizzly presentation/discussion I could find. I continued to look for grizzlies as my knowledge base increased. I began hiking in the backcountry and exploring new areas based on what I was learning from other people. I went on a field trip one day with Dr. Chuck Jonkle. During that one hike my knowledge base increased exponentially. I was hooked. My life goal now was to learn as much as I could about the "great bear."

Back in the 1980s, a sighting of a grizzly in the Lower 48 was rather rare. The formation of the IGBC, a partnership of federal and state agencies, was in response to the grizzly being listed as threatened under the, rather recent, Endangered Species Act. The IGBC's job was to come up with a plan to ultimately remove the bear from their threatened designation. I soon learned that I would have to hike more to learn more and have a better chance of seeing more grizzlies in the wild. At that time roadside sightings were uncommon. As a result, I started seeing grizzlies in areas where few people ventured. I began to see bears from the trail and even on the trail. I eventually learned the hard way-through my own experiences-that I needed to develop strategies and tactics to stay safe in grizzly country. I also realized that I needed to share my knowledge with other people in order to help both people and bears to coexist safely. My first two books and now this one are manifestations of this endeavor.

The purpose of this book is to bring together my experiences and the lessons that I have learned over the last 37 years, and which are largely based on the more than 50,000 miles I have hiked in grizzly country during that period. Many of my original thoughts on the subject have evolved over time, especially those pertaining to tolerant grizzlies. Some of my ideas (once they were established) have not changed.

I have basically remained firm on my original six principles that form the foundation of safe hiking in grizzly country. These are:

(1) Be able to recognize grizzly habitat.
(2) Be able to determine if a grizzly may be nearby.
(3) Make adequate noise.
(4) If a bear is encountered, freeze and remain calm, if possible.
(5) Judge how the bear is reacting to being in your presence.
(6) Carry, and be able to use bear spray.

Of these six, making noise and carrying bear spray are probably the most important. If the reader remembers nothing else, these two safety procedures will make up for many miscues when hiking in grizzly country. Hiking safely in grizzly country doesn't need to be "rocket science."

One of the most profound concepts I have come to understand is that I have a lot to learn. Some of my attitudes have changed due to continued new experiences. These new experiences have also revealed subtle behavior traits that I had never noticed. These revelations have had a profound effect on some of my previous bear theories. Most importantly those dealing with "habituated" grizzlies. The label "habituated" has usually implied something negative. Food conditioned bears are in a class by themselves. Other grizzlies, not those that associate people with a food reward, but that exhibit the acceptance of the presence of humans, I now refer to as "tolerant" grizzlies.

Tolerant grizzlies accept, and many even prefer the presence of people. They may even be using them for a number of reasons. It may not be people that cause a bear to become tolerant, nor is it some flaw in a grizzly that causes it to choose to be near people. Rather the grizzly, an unusually intelligent animal, will take advantage of opportunities it perceives as beneficial. The problem may be that we do not recognize or understand such behavior. I do not believe it is always a natural response for a grizzly bear to run from people.

This is an important concept. Just because one may be making a lot of noise doesn't mean one won't encounter a bear at close range. The main reason for making noise while hiking is to avoid surprising a grizzly. Making no noise or not enough noise has led to most maulings because the bear was surprised at a very close distance. However, making noise does not ensure that you won't encounter a grizzly, it just increases the chances that you won't put yourself in a situation where you could get mauled, because the bear knows you are there.

If you are making adequate noise and you still run into a bear, more than likely it is a tolerant bear. This does not mean you should abandon safe hiking principles. You should freeze and remain calm, and watch how the bear is reacting to your presence. Also, always keep your eyes on the bear. If you lose sight of a bear, you may encounter it again with possible negative results. A tolerant grizzly may look at you, but will return to whatever it was doing before you came on to the scene, which could include eating berries, or moving in a particular direction. Many tolerant bears may not even acknowledge your presence, but they still know you are there.

One situation where the bear may not be tolerant is when one is at or near a carcass. In this case, hopefully, you have your can of bear spray out and ready to use.

As more and more people recreate in grizzly country, more bears may appear to be tolerant. This does not mean hiking and encounter strategies should be ignored. Always respect grizzlies no matter how or where you encounter them. Carry bear spray, have it readily available, and know how to use it. I have had to use bear spray in two extreme encounters. It worked both times. However, I tell people that I do not want to put myself in a situation where I have to spray a bear again. Hopefully this book will give you enough information to avoid ever having to use it.

CHAPTER 1

FIRST ENCOUNTERS

All bear encounters are memorable, but first encounters are especially memorable for a number of reasons. First, they often provide a person with a new experience that is usually far different from any preconceived notions. Second, a person can learn a lot about themselves and how they react in potentially dangerous situations. Third, and most important, in my case anyway, you can do some real boneheaded things and still survive.

I classify the three encounters in this chapter as first encounters because of the newness of the situations to me and because of the important knowledge I gained and the mistakes I made. Ignorance is not bliss when it comes to hiking in bear country. Even though I had hiked extensively in bear country and had seen many bears prior to these encounters, I had not experienced a surprise meeting with either a black bear or a grizzly. Reading bear books made me aware of the risks but did not necessarily make me appreciate the full extent of all possible scenarios. I hope this book does a better job at preparing readers for bear encounters.

AUGUST 1989 - Apgar Lookout Trail, Glacier National Park

My wife, Suzi, and I had been camping in Glacier for five days. We had done much driving and hiking in the park, looking for bears without much success. It was a clear sunny day, and we decided to hike the Apgar Lookout trail. Our intention was not to look for bears. Instead, we wanted to hike the trail because we had never hiked it before and had heard the view from the top was outstanding.

The trail was about three miles long and climbed about 1800 feet in elevation. Once the trail starts to climb, it consisted of three long inclines divided by two switchbacks. We started the hike in the early afternoon, taking our time. We observed no bear sign on the way up. Except for a few huckleberry bushes with berries, there was nothing to indicate that bears might be in the area. When we reached the top, the views in every direction were breathtaking. We spent some time there, taking in the vista and relaxing in the sun. We then started a leisurely hike down to our truck.

Suzi was in the lead. We rounded the top switchback and began the middle descent. Halfway down, Suzi suddenly stopped, pointed, and said there was movement just ahead to the left of the trail. I immediately saw two small black shapes rocket up two separate trees. We knew what was happening. We started looking for the black bear mother in the dark underbrush, and then we heard a noise that neither of us had ever heard before. The best way to describe the noise, and the first thing I thought of when I heard it, is the sound of a hand saw cutting a dry 2x4 stud. It even had the same rhythm.

Now I could now see the mother bear at the base of the two trees cubs had shot up. My first thought was that she might be sick because of the strange sounds she was making. However, I soon realized she was making warning sounds. I would hear these sounds many times in the following years.

I now describe these warning sounds as "huffing," and both grizzlies and black bears make the sound. Some bear writers describe the sounds as "woofing," but the sounds are not like the "woofing" of dogs. Instead, they are like the alarm snorts of white-tailed deer, although not as nasal. A bear's "huff" is a distinct blowing sound.

As I continued to watch the mother bear, Suzi backed up the trail and disappeared around a bend. I took a few photos of the bear as it continued huffing. Then I backed up the trail to see where Suzi had gone. She had climbed a tree and was hoping for my return. Climbing a tree would not stop a black bear, but it made Suzi feel safe. I realized she had more sense and had recognized the danger. I, on the other hand, had been more interested in the bear's behavior than forming a correct response strategy. Black bears with cubs have mauled people and should not be taken lightly. I definitely made a mistake and only had the bear's patience to thank for a positive outcome. Her cubs were safely up trees, and I did not approach her. Had I pushed her due to my ignorance, events may have been different.

It was about six o'clock and we didn't want to spend any more time where we were. After waiting about 10 minutes I took out my bear spray and walked back down the trail to check on the bears. They were still there. The mother started huffing again, and the cubs were still in the trees. I went back to Suzi, and we decided to bushwhack down the mountainside to the lower section of the trail. We did this without much difficulty and finished our hike.

I basically look back at this encounter as a major learning experience. Little did I know that every encounter is a major learning experience.

NOVEMBER 1989 – Going-to-the-Sun Road, Glacier National Park

It was a mild fall and the Going-to-the-Sun Road that traverses the park was still open. My wife and I drove to a spot where a week earlier we had seen grizzlies digging. As we approached the area, I pulled over and scanned the open mountainside. Two grizzly siblings were digging in an open area. We drove up the road and stopped at a pullout. We were now about 300 yards below the bears. We got out of the truck, and as I was walked to the back of the truck to get my spotting scope and tripod, I heard a loud "huff." I now knew what that sound meant. I looked directly across the road to the sound, expecting to see a black bear. To my amazement, the sound came from a grizzly female with two cubs-of-the-year, only about 30 feet away. I turned to Suzi and said, as calmly as I could, "Get back in the truck."

I was astonished. That mother bear could have been on top of me in an instant before I ever knew what was happening. I began to decipher a revelation into the true nature of bears, and of grizzlies in particular. I never saw or had any indication there might be a bear that close when we got out of the truck. Looking at Photo 1 you can understand why. I took this photo after we got back into the truck, and I use this photo as an example of how people can be surprisingly close to a bear without being aware of its presence. People frequently hike by bears without ever knowing it. Many times, the bear, when it knows you are approaching, will hide until you are gone. Then it will continue doing what it was doing before you approached. This is why it is so important to make noise when hiking. I also look behind me every so often. Occasionally I have seen bears that I have just hiked past.

Photo 1

The grizzly bears seemed fairly tolerant, and they continued digging while people drove by or stopped. The cubs stayed near their mother and seemed unconcerned with anyone's presence. Importantly, no one got out of their vehicle, and it seemed this was the key to the bears' comfort zone near the road.

The event taught me that an encounter can occur in the unlikeliest places and when least expected. When hiking or recreating in bear country, the fewer preconceived ideas and expectations you have, the more appropriate your responses will be. In other words, when you are expecting *anything*, you will be less surprised and startled. Panic will be less likely, and more level-headed thinking will occur.

JULY, 1990 - West Side, Glacier National Park

I took a four-mile hike (one way) on the west side of Glacier to check on a huckleberry crop. I started the hike at 3 pm on a clear hot day, which was fairly typical for late July. About a mile and a half up the trail I encountered some rather productive huckleberry bushes with large, ripe berries. I couldn't resist; I began to gorge myself. As my hands turned dark purple from the berries, a couple of hikers approached and began to pick berries. After talking with them for a while, I continued my hike. The lower half of the trail where I had been picking berries was in a thick forest. I spotted some berry-filled scat on the trail, but it appeared old. About half way up the trail, the forest was cut with avalanche chutes. After about nine such chutes the trail broke into the open.

I sat down to cool off. I surveyed the surrounding huckleberry bushes and saw that the berries were not yet ripe at that elevation. I viewed the surrounding open areas and mountainsides without seeing any bears and decided it was time to head back. I was thinking about the area where I had picked berries. I figured I had time to pick more berries on the way down. As I neared the ripe berries in the forest, I noticed that the scat I had seen on the way up had either been pushed or scraped off the trail. The only explanation I could think of was that the hikers had kicked it off the trail. I continued hiking and soon rounded one of the many blind bends in the trail.

Right away I heard a loud "HUFF!" I looked up, expecting to see a black bear in the huckleberry bushes. To my complete astonishment, the sound came from a large grizzly. It was about 40 feet in front of me and just to the left of the trail. I was dumbfounded. I had heard and read that grizzlies were rarely seen in thick forest covers. Boy, did I have a lot to learn!

I grabbed the bear spray that was in my back pocket, pulled off the safety lever, and backed up the trail away from the grizzly.

The grizzly took off through the thick cover, not directly away from me but at an angle above me. I lost sight of it, but I could hear it crashing through the brush. I started climbing a nearby tree, thinking the bear could return and I wouldn't have much room on the trail to maneuver. I also would feel safer in the tree. As I was climbing, a branch rubbed across my face, flinging my glasses into space. Now I couldn't see a damn thing. As I moved higher in the tree, I heard a loud "huff" which scared the hell out of me and almost made me fall. Then I realized I had accidentally hit the trigger on the bear spray. I had been carrying the bear spray in one hand as I climbed the tree. Bear spray, when it goes off, sounds very much like the "huff" of a bear. I was lucky that I didn't spray myself in the face.

So there I was, about 20 feet high in a lodgepole pine, unable to see, wondering what to do next. Then dark clouds, thunder, and lightening approached. I said to myself, "Oh, this is great." I couldn't spend much more time in the tree. It was about 7 pm. There was plenty of daylight left, but the approaching storm and the need to locate my glasses dictated that I get the hell out of there.

I didn't know if the bear was still in the vicinity, and I couldn't see if it was. When I didn't hear any brush moving, I started yelling in hopes that if the bear was still around, the noise would encourage it to leave. After a few minutes of yelling, I climbed down the tree. I cautiously began searching for my glasses while staying alert to any noise or movement. Thankfully, I found my glasses rather quickly. I made a quick attempt to find the bear spray safety cover, but I didn't see it. I wanted to get out of there as quickly as possible.

I started hiking at a brisk pace, yelling the whole time. I didn't want to run into that same bear or any other bear for that matter. It started to rain, but luckily a big storm didn't materialize. I made it back to my vehicle in about half an hour.

I obviously made numerous mistakes on this hike. I acted like a typical tourist without a clue. Thanks to this bear's tolerance, nothing serious happened although I probably scared the heck out of the poor creature due to my lack of awareness and repeated yelling. Looking back on the encounter, valuable lessons can be learned.

First, an important clue was provided at the very beginning when I ran into the ripe huckleberries. If I could easily gorge on the berries, so could a bear. The scat in the trail was also an important sign. It told me a bear had been in the area. The scat appeared old, but combined with the presence of ripe berries, I should have realized that bears could certainly still be there.

Second, as I approached the berry area on the way down, I was not taking the proper precautions. I should have been making more noise and been more alert, especially when approaching blind curves in the trail.

Third, I assumed black bears were in thickly wooded areas. This was a totally false assumption, since grizzlies can be found anywhere, especially if food is available. Grizzlies are usually not seen in wooded areas simply because they are harder to see, not because they are absent. And when grizzlies are seen in wooded areas, they are usually at close range.

This bear encounter changed my thinking immensely. Ever since, I have tried to avoid having specific expectations and preconceived assumptions. The more I learn about bears the more I realize how much I don't know about bears. My hiking and personal response strategies are constantly changing as I gain new knowledge, especially from personal experience.

Thinking about all three of these "first encounters" has led me to believe I was a somewhat slow learner. Most people may not have the luxury of the bears' tolerance and patience. For some people, a first encounter could be their last. It is the purpose of this book to provide the reader with information, through my own experiences, to help you avoid these potentially dangerous situations.

CHAPTER 2

CHARACTERISTICS OF GRIZZLY COUNTRY

If you are preparing to hike in grizzly country, it is important to learn the components that make up grizzly habitat. There are many areas in the Western United States that still contain good habitat, but unfortunately, do not contain the number one component of grizzly country: the grizzly bear itself. For purposes of this book, I will only discuss the characteristics of where grizzlies already exist in North America, or may in the future. For example, all of western Montana should be considered grizzly country. Even though some areas have not seen grizzlies for a hundred years, the possibility still exists of running into one almost anywhere in the western part of the state. The same situation now applies to western Wyoming, some portions of Idaho and Washington, and most of Alaska. In Canada, all of the Yukon, the western portion of the Northwest Territories, western Alberta, and most of British Columbia should be considered grizzly country.

What makes these areas special is that many of the people there accept the presence of the great bear as an integral part of the ecosystem. Many of these people want to live in the last 'wild' places on earth.

Our attitudes will determine the survival of the grizzly as well as the continuing existence of wilderness. I would argue that the grizzly is not just a symbol of wilderness, but is actually the soul of wilderness. For me, wilderness is where grizzlies live. As I am writing this, I am witnessing a beautiful sunset over a federally designated wilderness area in Colorado. In my opinion, this is not real wilderness. There are no grizzlies in Colorado. It is, however, great grizzly habitat.

Most people would argue that it is poor grizzly habitat because there are too many people. I disagree. People didn't destroy the habitat; they destroyed the grizzly. They basically hunted down and killed every grizzly they could find. The food sources, the water, the cover and other characteristics for grizzly habitat are still there. It was the people's attitudes that determined the fate of the grizzly in many places, not the loss of the habitat.

What really is grizzly country? It is some of the most spectacularly beautiful country on the planet. It is home not only to the grizzly, but to clean water, clear air, healthy forests, abundant vegetation and other wildlife. It is in one word: exhilarating! It is accessible to people and for many it is home. It has always been home to both people and bears. Native Americans lived with the great bear for thousands of years. They respected and revered this magnificent animal. Wilderness was not perceived as a separate area. Grizzly country was their home. The bear was an intricate part of their lives and religion. It was, and is, a teacher. The grizzly has taught me incredible lessons of survival and tolerance. Every time I venture into grizzly country, I learn something new. In this context, we may be able to explore the characteristics of grizzly country in a more insightful manner.

FOOD

The word "food" has so many implications in grizzly country. It is both a key to the bear's survival and can be the cause to its demise. Present day people produce copious amounts of garbage. Sometimes they dispose of it properly, other times, not. Since people live and recreate in grizzly country, garbage can pose serious threats to the bear. A bear that gets into garbage or actually gets fed by people has the potential to become more than just a nuisance. Once a grizzly associates people with food rewards, it can become dangerous. Many grizzlies that get into garbage or are fed by humans end up being killed, either by wildlife officials trying to protect the public or illegally by people trying to protect property. A common phrase in grizzly country is, "A fed bear is a dead bear." It is of upmost importance that anyone recreating or living in grizzly country properly dispose of garbage and secure food and other attractants away from bears.

Abundant, naturally occurring food sources are the most important component of grizzly country. These take many forms. I still discover new food sources every year. Grizzlies are omnivores. They eat both meat and vegetation. One of the main tenants of safe hiking is the ability to recognize prime grizzly foods. The following list and descriptions to follow are certainly not all inclusive but should give the reader a basis for determining the possibility of an encounter. Hikers should always check with local authorities to determine what the grizzlies in that area are feeding on.

Berries: These include huckleberries (Photo 2) and blueberries, serviceberries, soapberries, chokecherries, raspberries, elderberries, kinnikinnick, mountain ash, rose hips, and certainly others.

Photo 2

Huckleberries and serviceberries are the main berry sources in the Northern Continental Divide Ecosystem (NCDE), which includes Glacier National Park and the Bob Marshall Wilderness Complex in Montana. In Alaska's Denali National Park and southwest Alberta, soapberries (also known as buffalo berries in some areas) are a main berry source.

Kinnikinnick (known as "bear berry" in Alaska) exists from Denali to Grand Teton National Park in Wyoming. These small berries are of prime importance. I have seen grizzlies eat kinnikinnick in late fall when other berries are gone for the year (Photo 3) and in early spring before other berries have appeared. Kinnikinnick berries can winter very well under deep snow. Because of this ability, and its widespread distribution, it is one of the most important yet underrated bear foods.

Photo 3

Roots: Many plants have edible roots. These include, but are not limited to, glacier lily, spring beauty, biscuit root, clover, and hedysarum. Where I live, glacier lily and biscuit root are the primary roots in the spring. In the fall, hedysarum and glacier lily roots are usually a good food source. I have seen biscuit root also used as a food source in the Greater Yellowstone Ecosystem in the spring, and I have seen hedysarum in Denali National Park in the middle of the summer. When determining whether grizzlies are eating any of these roots, look for "diggings"—areas where the ground has been dug up. With their long claws and massive shoulder muscles (as evidenced by their unique shoulder hump), grizzlies can excavate large areas. Diggings of most roots are fairly obvious.

Other vegetation: Grizzlies eat above-ground parts of many plants. These include equisetum (horsetail), cow parsnip, dandelions, grasses, clover, sedge, bear flowers, (which I have only seen in Denali), and the flowers of the glacier lily. I have never seen a grizzly eat cow parsnip after it flowers, but I have seen video of them doing so. In my experience, they prefer it during its early growth. Unlike diggings for roots, sometimes it is difficult to tell if a grizzly has eaten any of these plants. Therefore, if you see these plants, just assume a grizzly is in the area, especially in the spring when these plants are the most tender and nutritious.

Animals: A grizzly will eat just about any dead animal, including other bears and even humans. The grizzly is a natural scavenger. The grizzly will also kill to eat. It can and will kill just about any animal from the size of a vole to a full-grown elk or moose. This includes fish, especially in (but not limited to) Alaska (Photo 4). The larger the animal, the better the chance the bear will spend more time eating it, even sleeping on or near a carcass between feeding sessions. In many cases, grizzlies will bury the carcass under a mound of dirt and vegetation. This lessens the odor and thus lessens the risk of other bears or scavengers finding it. Because large animals are so nutritionally valuable, bears will often aggressively defend carcasses from other scavengers and perceived threats, including people. When hiking, be alert for strong odors (especially the smell of rotting meat) and look for coyotes, wolves, ravens, eagles, magpies, and seagulls. Unusual concentrations of one or more of these species in a small area is a good indication that a carcass is nearby with a grizzly bear ready to defend it. Either turn back or give these areas a very wide berth, making noise, having bear spray in hand, and using the other safety measures presented in this book.

Photo 4

WATER

Grizzlies love water. They swim in it, play in it, drink it, fish in it, and even use it for traveling (Photo 5). For the grizzly, water is both a source of hydration and a way to cool off in hot weather. In grizzly country, water is always nearby. When water is scarce (as in drought years) and during prime fishing seasons, some water sources can attract many bears.

Snow is also used for both cooling and hydration. Many times, I have seen bears using snow as a water source instead of bodies of water for no other reason than the snow was closer. Grizzlies love to play in the snow. Many times you can see marks where grizzlies have slid down snow-covered slopes.

No matter the physical form of water, extra care should be taken near water sources. When you are hiking near waterfalls or rushing streams and rivers, you must make extra noise so that

Photo 5

any nearby bear can hear you over the sound of water. Grizzlies may bed down in cool, shady, wet areas. A grizzly lying on a snowfield may look like nothing more than a large rock.

COVER

I consider cover to be anything that can conceal a grizzly bear from sight. This includes both natural and manmade features. When visibility is limited, special care must be taken. Making significant noise is absolutely required. The following types of cover are only a small part of what can be encountered in grizzly country.

Bushes and Tall Grass: Bushes can be food sources like huckleberries or simply a concealing plant like willows. In either case, they can be quite thick and large. I have seen huckleberry bushes four feet high and willows over my head. Even modest bushes are big enough to hide a sleeping grizzly or even one foraging. You may encounter large areas of dense bushes and tall grass along water ways and hill sides, including avalanche chutes. I know of people, including myself, that have walked right by grizzlies eating berries feet off the hiking trail. The same scenarios have occurred regularly in Katmai National Park. Of course, in each case, we were making noise so the bears knew we were there instead of being surprised, and they were tolerant bears that did not react negatively.

Thick forest or groups of trees: Grizzlies love to bed down in the shadows of trees, especially during the day. These temporary places to rest and sleep are called "day beds." Grizzlies like the thick shade for both its cooling effect and its concealment. These areas are even more desirable when both water and food are nearby. Also, grizzlies may drag carcasses into nearby trees to gain more solitude.

Rocky areas: These areas include cliffs, steep hillsides, and boulder fields. I have seen grizzlies bedded down at the tops of cliffs above hiking trails where they were not visible from the trails, but only from farther away. I have also watched bears, feeding on berries e.g., that simply walked behind large rocks and disappeared. Climbers and anyone hiking near or above timberline should be aware of possibly encountering grizzlies. These areas are a favorite for bears seeking hedysarum roots in the fall and army cutworm moths (another prime food source) starting in August.

Sagebrush: Sagebrush is a rather unique cover. It usually appears in large open areas where good visibility seems to stretch for miles. Such areas are deceiving. My friend, Jim Cole and I experienced the sighting of Jim's first Yellowstone grizzly in the middle of Hayden Valley in May 1994. Sagebrush is all over Hayden Valley. We were glassing with binoculars from one of the higher points in the valley when we spotted a grizzly in the sagebrush about 250 yards below us. It was digging, but for what? We did not have a clue. As the grizzly moved off, we decided to see what it had excavated. As we were hiking down the hillside from the east, we were able to keep our eye on the bear as it continued to move west. We thought we would be able to see the bear for a long time because it was moving through this large, open expanse. We hiked a bit lower and immediately lost sight of the bear. We quickly realized the entire valley was made up of small dips and swells - all nearly hidden by the sagebrush that was two- to five-feet high. Thinking that we could keep track of a bear in this environment was foolhardy. Bushwhacking called for much noise and deliberation. We reached the digging area and still could not determine what was being dug. Only later when we talked to another bear observer did we learn that the grizzly was digging for pocket gophers and their caches of seeds, a prime spring food source for grizzlies. We learned lessons on this hike: (1) when looking for grizzlies, open areas can be deceptive, and (2) sagebrush areas can be prime grizzly habitat despite appearances to the contrary.

Tundra: In many ways tundra presents the same problem as sagebrush. In Alaska, especially, the vast open areas are deceiving. The vegetation is anywhere between six inches to eight feet or more. Instead of sagebrush, you have grasses and dwarf bushes such as willow. Because of the vastness, it is hard to judge distances and thus the size of the vegetation. As in

Yellowstone's Hayden Valley, the tundra in Denali consists of rolling hills, swells, dips, and ridges. When Jim and I were there in 1994 conducting grizzly observations for the U.S. Biological Survey, we tried to hike on ridges as they provided the best footing and views. Yet even with radio telemetry, we still lost sight of radio-collared bears. It reinforced the fact that open landscapes can still hide bears.

TRAVEL CORRIDORS

People have travel corridors. We generally know them as trails, sidewalks, streets, roads, highways, rail systems, etc. They make getting from point A to point B easier and quicker, using the least amount of energy.

Grizzlies use travel corridors for the same reason. They use trails made by humans (Photo 6), themselves and by other animals. They use roads, both existing and abandoned, railroad tracks and rights-of-way and power-line clearings. Of course, they also use creeks, rivers, forest edges, ridge tops, lakes, and lake shores. You might say bears are like electricity: they both take the path of least resistance.

The result is that you can definitely run into a grizzly on a trail or a road. I've done it numerous times. When many people see a grizzly on the trail, they immediately think they are being stalked. More than once I have had to tell hikers to calm down as I explained that the bears use trails for the same reasons we do. There have been many grizzlies killed on railroads and highways because they were using them for ease of travel opportunities, but obviously with more risk. Anytime you use a geographic feature that makes your travel easier, it will make travel for a grizzly bear easier too. If clear areas make it easier to hike through a maze of downed trees or heavy brush, bears will use it too. Special attention needs to be focused on these "bear ways."

Photo 6

I've tried to point out the basic aspects of grizzly country that need to be recognized in order to increase the chances of a safe journey. If you are aware of what a grizzly considers important, you have more knowledge to avoid surprise encounters—and you will learn more about this animal and the real wilderness.

CHAPTER 3

MAKE NOISE

The best way to avoid encountering a grizzly is to make noise. Actually, that is not true. The best way to avoid encountering a grizzly is to stay out of grizzly country. However, most people would not even consider such an option. Many people visit grizzly country to see a grizzly, but most visitors simply want to experience the beauty and unique recreational opportunities such country provides. For those people, the thought of encountering a grizzly probably never enters their minds. Therefore, the first step in hiking safely in grizzly country is to become aware that the possibility—however small—of an encounter could occur. ***Making noise is the one tactic that offers the greatest protection against a negative encounter with a grizzly.***

Making noise will not guarantee that you will not run into a grizzly, but it will lessen the risk that you will surprise one at close range. Most maulings occur because the person walks right into a grizzly without any warning. The hiker ends up scaring the daylights out of the bear and the grizzly reacts instinctively to protect itself and/or its cubs. Making noise gives the bear a "heads up." If you are making appropriate noise, you may never even see the bear that has heard you coming. In many cases the grizzly runs away or "hides" until you have safely passed. In other cases, the bear merely goes about it's business such as eating berries or traveling.

The noise I usually make is loudly saying, "Hell-ooo," "yoo-hoo," or "yo." Sometimes I say, "hey Booboo." Many hikers say, "hey bear." The loudness and frequency vary, depending on the environmental conditions. Rushing water, wind, thick cover, and limited visibility usually dictate that I make louder and more frequent noise. Each hiker needs to use his or her own judgement. When in doubt, make more and louder noise.

When hiking alone I make noise on a fairly consistent basis. Since I believe that any encounter within 50 yards could turn into a serious situation, I make enough noise so that a bear can hear me from that distance.

If hiking with other people, especially three or more, the normal conversation generated is usually (but not always) enough to alert bears to your presence. Again, when in doubt make noise.

Whistling is not recommended since marmots (also known as whistle pigs) whistle, and grizzlies eat marmots. Also, most "bear bells" are not loud enough. Cow bells would be loud enough, but if they are clanging all the time, your hearing of other things around you would be severely affected. In other words, I do not recommend any whistles or bells for making noise.

The following situations illustrate the effect of making appropriate noise.

Eastside Glacier National Park - August 2007

My sister, Debby Nelson, and I decided to take a short evening hike. My wife, Suzi, and I had done this same hike earlier that day and saw a mother grizzly and yearling cub high above the trail. I felt we would have a good chance to see them again as the serviceberries in that area were abundant. As we started up the trail, we ran into a hiker coming down the trail. He stated that he had just seen a mother and cub further up the trail. We continued, making noise as we went.

Since there were intermittent thick bushes right next to the trail, I was making louder, more frequent noise. I was also hiking with my bear spray in my hand with the safety off. We climbed a steep portion of the trail. It began to level out when I caught a flash of brown approaching the trail about 20 feet to my left. I knew it was a bear even though I did not stop to look directly at it. I kept hiking at the same speed until I felt I was a safe distance away. I stopped and turned to see a mother grizzly and cub-of-the-year coming up to the trail. Debby, who was behind me as we hiked up the steep portion, had already stopped as she had seen the bears come towards the trail in front of her.

It was then, after seeing that the mother was not agitated with our presence, that I took out my camera and started taking pictures (Photo 7). The mother and cub crossed the trail between my sister and me and moved above the trail where they started eating the ripe serviceberries (Photos 8 and 9). As we watched and photographed the bears, more people came up and down the trail. Nobody freaked out. Some people took pictures or simply watched. Others continued hiking. The grizzlies slowly worked their way through the berry patches above the trail until they disappeared over a ridge.

I believe the key to this safe and amazing encounter was the fact that we were making appropriate noise. The mother grizzly knew we were coming. We did not surprise them even though we encountered them at very close range. In addition, everyone that was fortunate to see this family group acted in a responsible and calm manner, and the bears acted in a very tolerant way.

Photo 7

Photo 8

Photo 9

Eastside Glacier National Park - June 2008

I took an early morning hike to a beautiful lake. I was alone and all signs indicated I was the first person on the trail. The sun was to my back as I entered a semi-open area along the lakeshore. I had been making noise the whole way and continued to do so. I had taken this route two days earlier and had seen two grizzlies. One was a large male (it was mating season) and the other was what I presumed to be a female. The female had been digging glacier lily roots near the lakeshore in an area covered in thick brush. Making noise was a necessity. I also carried my bear spray in my hand the entire way.

I reached my destination without seeing any bears. I sat down in a fairly open area to glass the nearby mountainsides and soak up the warm morning sun. It was still fairly early.

I decided to head back to the trailhead and head home. I continued to make noise on the way back. I learned a long time ago that just because you do not see any bears on the way in, doesn't mean you won't see any on the way back. Also, the corollary is that just because you don't see any bears, doesn't mean there are none in the area.

About half way back as I rounded a sharp turn in the trail, I looked up and saw a grizzly walking right towards me on the trail. It looked like the female I had seen a couple of days earlier. If I backed up, I would lose sight of her. I had two options: (1) I could hold my ground and hope she would either turn back or she would leave the trail and go around me, or (2) I could get off the trail and hope she would walk by me and keep going. Since there was an open, albeit slightly steep slope for me to get off the trail, I did so.

I was able to get off the trail about 30 yards. The bear continued walking down the trail to where I had just been. Since she showed no sign of aggression, I decided to take some pictures. You can tell that she kept her eye on me as she passed (Photo 10). When she got a safe distance farther down the trail I climbed back up to It. I took a photo as she gave me one last glance (Photo 11). She then disappeared around the corner into thick brush where I presumed she dug glacier lilies. At this point I continued back to the trailhead and my vehicle. Before I left for home, I stopped at the ranger station and left a note for the local bear ranger letting him know what happened. I thought he might want to "post" the trail so other hikers would know of the bear on or near the trail.

By making noise I believe the grizzly was alerted to my presence. I did not surprise her when I rounded the corner on the trail. I felt that since she knew I was on the trail, she was able to remain calm. I also believe that moving below the

Photo 10

Photo 11

trail and giving her room to go past made her more tolerant of my presence.

Eastside Glacier National Park - August 2013

I took a hike in the same area described immediately above. This time I was hiking with Shane Conner, a wildlife biologist and fellow bear enthusiast. It was a morning hike on a clear, beautiful day. We were not the first ones on the trail. We knew this because we met a couple on their way back. They stated that they just observed a grizzly near the trail a few hundred yards ahead of us. Because of the time of year and the fact that I observed many ripe serviceberry patches near this trail a couple of days earlier, I figured the bear was in the area eating the berries.

Shane and I continued on the trail, making noise with our bear sprays in hand. I was in the lead. We hiked deliberately, inspecting every nook and cranny along the trail. We reached our destination without seeing or hearing the bear. When bears are eating berries, they sometimes can be heard moving through the brush. They aren't trying to be quiet. We stopped and glassed the open areas without spotting any bears. After a few more minutes we decided to head back to the trailhead.

As we hiked back, we were just as deliberate as on the way in. We continued to make as much noise and still had our bear sprays out. This time Shane was in the lead. As we passed a group of serviceberry bushes, I heard some brush move a little behind and to my left. Without breaking stride or stopping I took a quick glance towards the sound and was slightly surprised to see a grizzly about ten feet off the trail, eating serviceberries. I turned towards Shane and said, "Hey Mono (his nickname), you just walked right by a grizzly." Of course, so did I. If that bear had not made any noise or if I had not heard it, we would have walked past without seeing it, even though it was only a few feet away.

We hiked a little farther, stopped, and turned around just as the grizzly stepped on the trail and walked away from us. The grizzly then moved above the trail into a large open area. We walked back up the trail to take some photos as the grizzly fed on berries and slowly made its way up the mountainside. (Photo 12)

Once again, making noise was the key to a safe encounter. The grizzly remained calm and was totally tolerant of our presence. In all of my years of hiking in grizzly country I have only had (thank God!) two severe encounters. Both could be directly attributable to the lack of making appropriate noise.

Photo 12

Glacier National Park - June 2018

I try to start my hikes early in the morning. The rising sun offers great light, especially for photography. The colors are saturated, the water of calm lakes and pools offer mirror like effects, and the air is usually crisp and clear. I also want to be the first one on the trail, although this is becoming increasingly difficult because of the rise in number of visitors.

This morning, I was on the trail before 7 a.m. I did not see any others on the trail. My destination was the top of a rock outcropping from which I had a 360-degree view of a large valley surrounded by open mountainsides. I made noise and carried my bear spray out with the safety off the entire way without any incident. I reached the top and immediately spotted a mother grizzly and two light colored yearlings far off in the distance. I watched them for about a half hour through my binoculars. They appeared to be turning over rocks for insects and grubs. It was then I decided to hike back along the trail to a nearby lake. I wanted to take video and I would be closer. I also did not have my tripod and there were trees along the shore that I could use to steady my camera.

As I was taking video, I saw the bear family make a distinct move down towards the opposite side of the lake. The trail went right through a thick stand of lodge pine right next to that shore. I quickly realized if I did not start hiking back immediately, I might run into them in those trees. I started back. I made a lot of noise and, of course, had my bear spray out.

I made it through the trees and to an open area with a small beach. At about the same time a group of hikers came up the trail. When they stopped, I asked them if they had seen the bear family and they replied that they had not. We waited a few minutes to see if the bears would appear at the lake. The hikers decided to keep going, making noise as thy went. They also had bear spray and knew how to use it. I decided to head back to the trailhead. I had a good hunch that the grizzlies could soon appear. It was imperative that I made plenty of noise.

I rounded a jog in the trail, looked up at a very close cliff band, and saw the mother and one of the cubs looking down at me. I immediately froze and realized that they had heard me. Since they exhibited no agitation, I took some photos (Photo 13). The mother and cub moved ahead of me down towards the trail. I soon saw the other cub following close behind (Photo 14). The bear family moved through some thick cover and popped out on the trail about 50 yards in front of me (Photo 15). They leisurely walked down the path and disappeared into more cover towards the lake.

Photo 13

Photo 14

Photo 15

I doubled back to the beach where I had better visibility. They soon appeared on the edge of the lake about 200 yards away and began slowly walking along the shore away from me. I decided to leave the area given the bears were now much farther from the trail. As I headed back, making noise with my bear spray out, I began to encounter other hikers. I told each group that a grizzly with two cubs were in the area. Some people made noise, others did not. Some people had bear spray, some did not. I have no idea if the bears were seen or encountered again.

This family of grizzlies seemed very tolerant. Given the amount of people that hike this trail, it is really not a surprise. Some days during the summer this particular trail, and others nearby can see up to a thousand hikers a day. These trails and others throughout Glacier are getting more crowded every year. I believe that the grizzlies in these areas could see more people per day than anywhere on the planet. No matter how tolerant grizzlies appear, proper safe hiking strategy should be employed, especially making noise.

CHAPTER 4

CARRY BEAR SPRAY!

I cannot overemphasize the importance of carrying bear spray when hiking in grizzly country. Since the development and availability of bear spray in the early 1980's, the majority of the people killed by grizzlies were not carrying it. I know of no incident where a person that was able to successfully deploy bear spray in time was seriously mauled or killed. Of course, this implies that one must not only carry bear spray, but must have it readily available and know how to use it. Carrying bear spray in the bottom of your pack, for example, is worthless. It must be in hand or available in an instant. Grizzlies are unbelievably quick.

I have met people on the trail who are carrying bear spray in unusual places on their person and/or have never taken the safety off. One example occurred in August of 2019 in Glacier Park. I met some hikers while I was near a large open mountainside looking for bears eating berries. I noticed that one hiker had his bear spray on a carabiner hooked to the side of his backpack. I briefly mentioned the incidents later in this chapter. I asked him how fast he could get his spray out. He proceeded to do this. I immediately said, "you're screwed." When I say it must be available in an instant, I mean it. Another time, I asked a member of a small group I was training to take the safety off of an empty can. To my surprise she took the can, pointed it directly at her face, and took the safety off. I laughingly said, "don't ever do that again." People need to be educated properly to use bear spray effectively. In most cases this never happens.

There at least 4 bear sprays on the market that are registered with and approved by the Environmental Protection Agency. Only use bear spray with such approval. The EPA registration number will be on the can.

I recommend bear sprays with a spray distance of at least 25 feet and a spray duration of at least six seconds. Without such properties, I probably would not have experienced a successful outcome when I sprayed the grizzly that attacked Jim Cole in Glacier, described later in this chapter. The only bear spray that I carry is Counter Assault Bear Spray. I have been doing so since 1985. It meets or exceeds the above distance and duration specifications mentioned above, as do one or more other brands. I cannot recommend other brands, though, as I have never used any other brand.

All bear sprays work the same way. The "trigger" is protected by a safety cover to prevent accidental discharge. Many people, if they have not practiced, cannot remove the safety or do it in an unsafe manner, as mentioned above. ***The most important thing to learn is how to remove the safety quickly and effectively.*** Depressing the trigger and spraying is similar to operating some household and industrial propellants, so people usually have some experience with that feature.

The best way to learn how to use bear spray is to practice with training canisters from Counter Assault and other manufacturers. Training cans should only be used outside, as the propellant can be irritating to the eyes and throat. If no training canister can be obtained, then I recommend using a can of real bear spray. With the wind to your back in an open area far away from any structures, cars, pets, and people, flip off the safety and fire a short burst. Using a real can in this manner will give you an idea of how to remove the safety and see the spray pastern, and still have enough contents in the can to use while hiking (bear sprays have expiration dates; if you need to buy a new can, use the old can for practice). It is important to remember that the spray disperses and will not be visible after a short time, but can still cause irritation.

I have had to use bear spray in two extreme situations. I emphatically attest to its efficacy.

Glacier National Park - September 29, 1993

Jim Cole and I started on a 25-mile day hike at 7:30 on a beautiful fall morning. Our destination was the Fifty Mountain area 12.5 miles away. We reached the area about noon. We had not seen fresh grizzly sign on our way in, but here were numerous fresh diggings of glacier lily roots. We ate lunch and glassed the open areas for grizzlies without any luck. We thought they might be bedded down on the warm fall afternoon. At 2pm. we decided to head back.

Jim led on the way. I stopped and scanned open areas wherever there was a good view, then caught up with Jim until I stopped again. After about two miles, as I was catching up to Jim for maybe the third time, I heard a loud, long "Hissss" like a locomotive letting off steam. Even though I was looking down at the trail, watching my footing, I knew what we had run into. My first thought was "Here we go."

When I looked up the grizzly was charging Jim and almost on top of him. I was about 45 to 50 feet away. I yelled at Jim, "Hit the ground!" He didn't have a choice. At the same instant he was heading for the dirt, the grizzly was swiping at him with its right front paw. However, since Jim was falling down and away from the bear, the grizzly was missing him.

I had always wondered how fast I could get my bear spray out if the need arose. I carried it on my pack belt. I pulled it out of its holster so fast I amazed myself. I pulled the safety off and took two steps backwards on the trail, waiting for the grizzly to charge me. Everything that I had ever read up to that time indicated that when a grizzly is confronted with multiple threats, the bear will focus on the closest threat and then go for the next. I was the next. By this time Jim was face down on the ground and the grizzly was standing on top of him.

The first bite was right to Jim's head. The grizzly ripped his scalp wide open. Jim instinctively put his left hand above his head as a defensive move. The grizzly bit right through his wrist, breaking it. The bear then bit Jim's left hip. This could have been the most disabling injury, but Jim carried his camera in a hip case and the bear ended up biting into the camera. All of this happened very fast. It then dawned on me that the grizzly did not know I was there.

I began walking towards the grizzly, which had its back towards me. From about 40 feet away I aimed the spray at the bear and fired a short burst. The grizzly heard the "whoosh" of the spray, looked up, saw me, and charged. I held down the spray trigger all the way and didn't let up. I sprayed at the grizzly's face as it came at me. I could see the charging bear through the spray's reddish-orange mist. The bruin took a full blast of the red-hot-pepper derivative directly in its face. The grizzly suddenly stopped 5 feet in front of me, turned, and ran down the mountainside. It disappeared out of sight.

Jim was still lying on the ground. I asked him if he was alright. He responded that he was okay. He stood up and walked up the trail about 60 yards to some shade. By the time I reached him, he had opened his pack, pulled out his first aid kit, and dumped the contents on the ground. It was then that

I saw the profuse bleeding from the open gash on his head.

I found the hydrogen peroxide and poured it into the head wound. I placed all the first aid items containing gauze on the wound. Then I opened my pack and retrieved a clean, white, long-sleeved shirt and wrapped it tightly around Jim's head. I used an ace bandage to tightly wrap the shirt. Next, I treated his wrist.

Our adrenaline was pumping, especially Jim's. We had 10.5 miles to get back to the trailhead and only about 4 hours of daylight left. Jim did not want to spend the night while I went for help. We packed up and left. We had a few minor delays on the way back due to rearranging packs and the onset of fatigue, but luckily, we made it to our vehicle just as it was getting dark.

I drove to the nearest phone to call 911 so they could alert the Kalispell Regional Medical Center to prepare for our arrival. We got to the hospital about 45 minutes later. After an initial examination, Jim went into surgery for both his head wound and wrist. The surgery was successful, and Jim healed over the winter without any long term affects. The next summer we volunteered with the National Biological Survey and did extensive observational studies in Denali National Park. The mauling had no effect on Jim's or my passion for grizzlies.

I learned a great deal from this incident. First, bear spray works. As a matter of fact, the thought that it might not work never entered my mind as the grizzly charged. Second, since the mauling, I always carry two cans of bear spray on my pack belt. I emptied most of my can during the attack. If a similar situation should ever arise, I want a backup can available. Third, if there are two or more people in your group, at least two people should be carrying bear spray. Jim carried bear spray on his pack belt. However, he had no chance to get it out because of the speed of the attack. If I had not had bear spray, what would I have done? I don't even want to think about it. Fourth, whenever I am in questionable situations, I now carry one in hand with the safety off. If Jim would have been doing this, I believe he would have had a good chance to spray the attacking grizzly. Of course, one has to be careful not to accidentally discharge the spray when carrying it in this manner.

After many years of reflecting on this incident, I have come to many conclusions about our actions and those of the grizzly. First, we scared the ever-loving shit out of that bear. Before we left the attack scene, I investigated the area from which the bear had exploded. There was a slightly dug out area about 10 feet off the trail in a small group of trees. I firmly believe that Jim walked right next to a bedded down, sleeping bear and woke it up. It was a classic case of a surprise encounter at close range, and the bear reacted in a predictable manner. If we had been making proper noise, we likely, would never have seen the bear. It probably would have moved away as we approached. Also, If we would have stayed together, we probably would have been talking to each other and making enough noise. However, we were effectively each hiking alone because of my frequent stopping to look for grizzlies while Jim kept hiking, and my focus was in the distance rather than where it should have been: closer to where we were hiking.

Also, because we saw no fresh sign in the area on the way in, we let our guard down on the way back. We really didn't think there could be a bear that close to the trail we had just hiked on. Never assume that since you didn't see a bear or any bear sign on the hike in, that there isn't one close by. This incident proves that point. It also proves that having bear spray readily available and having the ability to use it properly under duress can sometimes make up for faulty assumptions and mistakes.

Glacier National Park - August 17, 1999

I was on a hike to an observation point on a cliff overlooking a large valley right below the westside of the Continental Divide. It was about 7:30 on a clear, cool morning. I neared my destination, which was about 200 yards off the main trail at about 9:50. As I approached the cliff, I noticed fresh diggings of glacier lily roots. I carefully looked around and listened intently for any indication of a nearby grizzly, but I saw and heard nothing. I continued to the edge of the 50-foot cliff where I took off my pack and sat down to glass the valley below.

When I took off my pack, I also took one of the cans of bear spray out of its holster and laid it on the ground next to me. I do this whenever I sit down for any length of time. I had a lot of area to glass, and I figured I would be there for a while. I scanned the entire valley with my binoculars for about 20 minutes without seeing anything. I took out my food bag and had breakfast, consisting of dry food, along with a sports drink in my water bottle.

I continued glassing. At about 10:40 am I heard something behind me. I quickly looked around and came face to face with a mule deer doe that was watching me from about 20 feet away. A little later I decided to move to a higher elevation where I could see more territory.

I stood up and started packing to leave. As I bent down to put my food bag into my pack, I noticed a flash of brown out of the corner of my eye. I looked up and saw a female grizzly with a yearling cub coming around a small group of trees about 20 yards away. She saw me at almost the same instant, and she immediately charged!

My only thought was, "I hope that can of bear spray that I put on the ground next to me is at my feet when I look down." I had another can of spray in a holster on my pack belt, but knew I didn't have time to lift up the pack and get that can. I looked down and there, thank God, was the can I had placed on the ground. I reached down and grabbed it. As I pulled off the safety I said in a loud, low voice, "NOoo...!" I intended to say "NO, don't come any closer," but "NO" was all I got out.

The two grizzlies promptly stopped and stood up. The cub did exactly what the mother did. They were both huffing. I thought it was kind of cute. It was as if the cub was trying to be a tough guy, saying, "Oh boy, Mom, we're going to nail this guy." It was a ridiculous thought, but I have learned that in life-threatening situations, when things are happening very fast, the mind does not operate in the "normal" fashion.

The standing bears were about 20 feet away. I could clearly see the females' six swollen teats. She came down on all fours towards me and I instantly triggered a short burst of bear spray at her face. The cloud of spray headed straight towards her, but in the strong wind (the wind had come up while I had been sitting on the cliff) it made a 90 degree turn before it got to her. Luckily, the "whoosh" sound from the can and the red cloud of spray startled both bears and again they slammed on the brakes.

Both grizzlies started moving laterally to my right. As they were moving, I glanced down the cliff. Suddenly I realized I could climb down it. In all my previous visits to this cliff, I never thought it could be climbed, but now a few, small, possible footholds looked like a stairway to me. So, I started to climb down, all the while facing the bears. There is no guarantee that bear spray will work 100 percent of the time. If it didn't work this time, I was going to bail off the cliff. However, I really didn't want to abandon my pack because there was food in it, and I was afraid the bears would get into it with dire consequences for them and possibly other hikers in the future.

The mother grizzly came towards me again. About 10 feet away she stopped and stood up. Now I had to look up at her because I had already moved down the cliff to the top of my knees. I wasn't going to wait for her to come down. I triggered the spray and this time, because of the short distance and favorable wind direction, the spray hit her directly in the face. In a flash, she and her cub were gone.

I could hear her huffing and puffing as they ran towards the trail. Unfortunately, they were headed in the same direction I had to go! I climbed on top of the cliff, gathered my things, and without delay I started towards the trail. I wanted to get out of there. I pulled out my other can of bear spray and took off the safety. I walked deliberately and alertly with a can of bear spray in each hand and yelling, "Yo bear! Hey bear!" I did not see the grizzlies again as I reached the trail and hiked to the nearest park facility to report the encounter.

This incident shows that there are different ways encounters can occur. In the incident with Jim, humans "ran" into a grizzly. In this episode grizzlies "ran" into a human. But both incidents had one main factor in common: The humans didn't make enough noise to alert the bears that humans where there. I firmly believe that both encounters could have been avoided with proper noise.

However, in the last incident I'm not sure that making constant or loud noises while sitting in a prime wildlife viewing area is conducive to the well-being of the animals being observed. A better tactic in such a situation would be to stay more alert and look all around on a consistent basis. Most of my time was spent focused on the valley below me and not behind or to the sides of me. It was fortunate that I had a can of bear spray on the ground next to me. It shows that bear spray must be readily available to be used effectively.

As stated previously, since the first incident, I now carry two cans of bear spray on my pack belt. Both cans of spray are in front, on my pack belt, where they can be easily reached. They are in the same place when I wear my typical backpacking or long day-hiking arrangement. I often carry one can in my hand with the safety off, especially when hiking

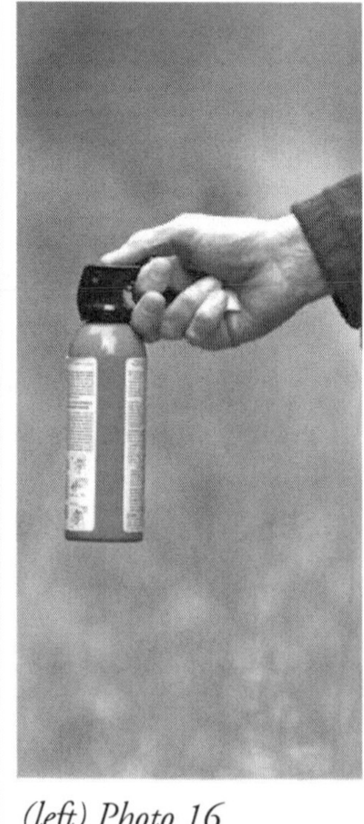

(left) Photo 16
(right) Photo 17

alone or in tight spots with limited visibility. Photos 16 and 17 show how I do this (these photos were taken by my wife, Suzi). Obviously, one must be very careful not to accidentally discharge the spray when carrying it this way.

I want everyone who hikes in grizzly country to carry and know how to properly use bear spray, even in areas where bears may appear to be extremely tolerant, or if people say you don't need it. Not only is it important for one's own safety, but it can also save the lives of grizzlies by preventing serious or deadly maulings of people. In such cases, authorities usually feel the necessity to kill the "offending" bear even though it is usually the victim's fault for not following safe hiking protocols.

One last point that should be discussed: only use bear spray on charging bears or bears that are close and very agitated. Signs of agitation are huffing a great deal, clacking jaws together, drooling, and/or bouncing up and down with the front legs. Even in these situations backing up and/or talking softly, may calm the bear down. Never spray a bear that is just standing still and looking at you, if it is not displaying any of the above behaviors. In some cases where the bear is deliberately approaching, yelling a loud "NO" may suffice to stop it.

Employing safe hiking strategies and tactics, as presented in this book will, hopefully, help people avoid situations where they actually have to use bear spray. I never want to be in a situation where I have to use it again. It is not fun.

CHAPTER 5

REMAIN STILL AND CALM

Probably the single most important action to take when a bear is encountered is to freeze and remain still and calm while watching the bear's reaction to your presence. I have learned that in order to make the right decisions in bear encounters, you must first determine if the bear reacts negatively to you or your group. The bear's reaction will then determine what you do next, what I call your "personal response strategy." Remaining still and calm during this initial process helps you act more rationally and may help the bear decide that you are not a threat. In addition, remaining still (holding your ground) even in cases where the bear moves towards you sometimes indicates to the bear that you cannot be intimidated.

August, 1992 - West Side, Glacier National Park

Jim Cole and I took a hike on the west side of Glacier to explore new country. We started very early in the morning to reach a good viewing location along a high ridge by sunrise. Much of the hike was off trail. Huckleberry bushes were just starting to turn red, and as the sun rose on the ridge, their brilliant colors became evident. We felt we had a good chance to see a grizzly or two that day, especially since the "hucks" were ripe all the way to the top of the ridgeline.

We came to the edge of a small side canyon that cut into the ridge. I was leading when we started down the steep embankment towards the bottom of the canyon. In the thick cover below and to our left, we suddenly heard an incredible thrashing and crashing. Of course, our first thought was a grizzly, but we saw a huge bull moose running away from us, crashing through the alders and huckleberry bushes. We decided we had probably spooked the moose, but we were aware a grizzly also could have scared it.

I continued down the steep bank with my bear spray in hand and the safety off. As I reached the very bottom of the cut, I heard a huffing sound, and it was getting closer. The sound was like an approaching steam locomotive, and it was coming from the area where the moose had been spooked. This time we knew it was a grizzly. I stood my ground at the bottom of the narrow canyon and faced the sound. Jim remained still on the side of the embankment. I remained calm with my bear spray in my outstretched hand, pointing at the direction of the huffing. There was nothing else to do but wait. We didn't want to make noise because we could tell the bear was already stressed.

The grizzly tore out of the brush on a straight run about 40 yards in front of me. When it saw me, it did not break stride but turned to its left and continued into the thick brush. There was still a huffing sound coming from the same area. It was another bear. I remained still while the second grizzly came into the open. This bear was larger, and when it saw me, it stopped dead in its tracks and took what seemed like a good long look at me. Then it followed the slightly smaller bear into the thick brush and disappeared. For a second, I thought the second bear might charge after it stopped. However, having the option of using the bear spray, which I had ready, I did not feel threatened or scared.

In a few seconds everything was still. Jim came down and we immediately started up the other side of the cut. We did not feel safe at the bottom of the small canyon. When we reached the top on the other side, we discussed what had just happened. We both realized we had encountered a female grizzly with a two-year-old cub. The bears either spooked the moose or vice versa, or we spooked the moose and the moose spooked them. The fact that the mother was behind the cub indicated that the threat she perceived was behind them and not in front of them where we were. In any case they wanted to get to a new area really fast. Unfortunately, I was in their way.

In this encounter, I felt both Jim and I did the right thing. Actually, I'm not aware of any other alternatives. The event reinforced my main concept of freezing and remaining calm as the important first act in a bear encounter.

May, 1994 - South Side, Glacier National Park

Jim and I decided to make two hikes in one day on the south side of Glacier. We reached the first trailhead in the early morning. Our objective was a nearby mountain to check on abundant glacier lilies there. We reached the summit without seeing any bears. On the way down we bushwhacked off trail. About halfway down we spotted a black bear at the bottom of an avalanche chute. After viewing this bear, we descended without seeing any other bears.

For our afternoon hike our ultimate destination was a place where we had seen a large male grizzly the previous spring. We planned to pass the bottom of the same avalanche chute where we had seen the black bear earlier in the day. As we approached the chute, we were quiet but cautious and alert. The moment we reached the edge of the chute, where we could see to the bottom of it, we spotted what we assumed was the same black bear. We were much lower and therefore much closer than we had been earlier. We studied the bear for a while, trying to determine what it was eating. Then we continued into the chute. We noticed it was filled with bright yellow glacier lilies and thick willows and alders. Our goal, however, was to explore a biscuitroot hillside another mile up the trail.

Jim was in the lead when we reached the other side of the chute. I was looking down, watching my footing, when all of a sudden Jim said, "Tim—there is a large grizzly right in front of us on the trail." The grizzly was about 40 yards away. Of course, we both froze in our tracks. I had been carrying my bear spray with the safety off because of the thick cover in the chute. The bear looked at us, moved off the trail, and circled above us. He traveled to a small knob about 35 yards away. By this time Jim and I had our cameras out.

The bear stopped, stood up, and looked at us (Photo 18). The bear did not seem accustomed to humans. However, he seemed to have the attitude that we were not going to intimidate him in his territory. He simply came down and slowly ambled off in the opposite direction from where we were going.

We continued hiking without seeing another bear. On the way back we made plenty of noise to make sure that we did not run into the large grizzly again.

One vitally important aspect when hiking is to never lose sight of the bigger picture. We spent a lot of time that day concentrating, for whatever reason, on one black bear to the exclusion of what we were really looking for—grizzlies. We may have let our guard down by thinking that a black bear would not be so calm if a grizzly was nearby. Well, that theory proved wrong. Anything is possible, and hikers should be adequately prepared when it comes to the behavior of bears.

Photo 18

Our hiking strategy was valid. I had the bear spray out, but I would have had it out in any case because of the thick cover. Being in a state of high alert whenever you travel through thick cover cannot be emphasized enough. In any case, things worked out, as in most encounters. The bear left without incident, albeit not in the normal fashion (i.e., running). Our encounter strategy was also valid. We froze and watched the bear's reaction to us. The bear's reaction dictated that we could think about taking pictures.

September, 1996 - West Side, Glacier National Park

Jim Cole and I took a day hike to check various areas between 6000 and 7000 feet for huckleberries. As we approached 5,500 feet, ripe huckleberries appeared on the bushes. As we approached 6000 feet, the berries became abundant. It looked like a good day for spotting grizzlies.

We arrived at our main lookout and immediately saw grizzlies below us and at a distance, foraging on huckleberries. We observed their behavior for some time and decided to check other areas. We spotted a female grizzly and yearling cub foraging on huckleberries, watched them for a while, and then went back to our main lookout.

As we were approaching the lookout, we saw a female grizzly and two yearlings running away from us into the trees. When we got closer to our observation area, we ran into this same family group again. At this point we were about 40 yards away. We immediately froze, remained calm, and watched how the bears reacted to us. The cubs immediately ran in the opposite direction and disappeared behind a group of trees. The female held her ground between us and her cubs and watched our reaction to her (Photo 19). She looked towards the cubs, then looked back at us. Upon realizing we were not a threat, she turned and ran after her cubs.

Once again, we had an encounter that ended with the bears running away. However, this situation could have been far different if we had reacted in a different manner. For example, if we had started hollering or waving our arms in the air, rather than remaining still and calm, the mother might have perceived us as a threat and charged. Of course, if the cubs had been between us and her, or, in the worst-case scenario, if we had been between her and her cubs, the situation definitely would have been more challenging.

April, 2000 – Going to the Sun Road, Glacier National Park

It was a beautiful, warm, sunny spring day and I was biking on the Going to the Sun Road. I started where the gate closed the road to vehicles near the head of Lake McDonald.

Many cars were in the parking area; a lot of people had the same idea.

About 1.5 miles into my journey, I looked up and saw a grizzly about 100 yards ahead of me, walking towards me on the road. No one else was around. I got off my bike and started taking photos (Photos 20 and 21). The bear was aware of my presence but kept coming. As it approached, it moved to the creek side of the road. It looked as if it would come within 10 yards of me, or closer, if I did not move. When it was about 35 yards away and still approaching, I turned my bike sideways in front of me. The bear immediately changed direction, headed for the opposite side of the road, and disappeared into heavy cover (Photos 22). I never saw it again.

It was a radio-collared bear and probably somewhat tolerant. It had probably just moved down from its winter den and was on its way to a snow-free area. The road was the

Photo 19

Photo 20

Photo 21

easiest way to travel, allowing the bear to conserve energy. As I learned later, many people saw the bear on the road.

It probably would have passed me on the road if I had not changed position. However, that was a risk I was not going to take without sending some message to the bear. Moving my bike in front of me while standing my ground provided some minimal protection and probably sent the bear a message. The bear either saw that movement as a sign of dominance or as an unknown situation that experience had not yet taught it how to handle. Another possibility was that the bear always reacted that way with people that turned their bike sideways. In any case, the bear did not become agitated or aggressive. It just changed its route.

Photo 22

CHAPTER 6

KEEP YOUR EYES ON THE BEAR

Being able to make the right decision to avoid an encounter (for example, when a bear is seen at a distance) or to safely survive an encounter depends in most cases of knowing exactly where the bear is. Even though large, a grizzly bear is adept at disappearing into its surroundings. Notice in the following situations the importance of keeping ones' eyes on the bear.

Glacier National Park, August, 1992

It was a very unusual late August day. A freak snowstorm had dumped a foot of snow in the area where Jim Cole and I were hiking. The huckleberries were just beginning to ripen over a wide area. As we gained elevation towards our destination, we were surprised to see numerous bear tracks in the snow. The tracks were heading up the trail in front of us. First, we saw black bear tracks, and as we got even higher, we began to see grizzly tracks. The tracks were made by more than just a couple of bears.

Over the years Jim and I have located many observation spots throughout the ecosystems we have studied. One of the first such lookouts was our destination on this hike. From this cliff we had seen grizzlies digging glacier lily roots in the spring and eating huckleberries in the fall. On this particular day we were about to see an amazing display of bear behavior. We would see a total of 13 black bears and 8 grizzlies. All of the bears were eating huckleberries. Everywhere we looked we saw bears. The bears seemed to be aware that after a snow, berries turn to mush and fall off within a few days. The bears came "out of the woodwork" to eat as many berries as possible before there were no more to eat.

Of all the bears we saw that day, there were two that particularly intrigued us, a female grizzly and what appeared to be either a two-year-old cub or a rather large yearling. We first spotted these bears eating "hucks" about 250 yards below us. We continued to observe them as they came within 50 yards of us right below the cliff (Photo 23). They were not aware of our presence. That is one of the reasons why we use

Photo 23

this particular spot so much: bears rarely know we are there. Right after I took the photograph, the two bears seemed to disappear into thin air. One minute they were right below us and the next minute they were gone. We spent the next five minutes walking along the edge of the cliff hoping to spot them again, but without success. I finally turned and looked behind us and there they were (Photo 24), lying down watching us. They were probably wondering, "What are those two dim wits doing over there?"

Photo 24

Somehow the bears had found a slot in the cliff, climbed up and circled around behind us without our being aware of their movements. This is an important example of why you should never take your eyes off a grizzly until you can safely leave the area. If you lose sight of a bear, you never know where it is likely to turn up. You could end up running right back into it. The fact that the bears lay down and watched us speaks volumes about their incredible curiosity and intelligence.

Great Bear Wilderness, August, 1992

Jim and I decided to explore a new area in the Great Bear Wilderness, which lies just south of Glacier National Park. From a distance I had previously seen grizzlies on a ridge in the area. On this hike we were going to hike directly into the ridge area.

It was a beautiful sunny day right before Labor Day weekend. As we climbed in elevation, the views were fantastic. We could see a beautiful crystal-clear lake below us and towering mountains with hanging glaciers all around us. We reached the first saddle in a high ridge and bushwhacked along the ridge until we found a good observation point. We sat down and began viewing the open slopes around us. We ended up spotting four black bears over two hours. The bears appeared to be eating huckleberries and mountain ash. We backtracked to the first saddle and then continued on the loop trail.

We hiked through a high mountain basin full of huckleberries and spotted fairly fresh grizzly berry scat, but no bears. We continued on the trail around another saddle, and it was then that I saw bear tracks in the dust on the trail. The tracks were headed away from us. However, due to the dry conditions, we were unable to determine their age. We began climbing slowly towards another saddle and as we approached, I looked at the peak directly to the south and spotted a promising avalanche chute. As we hiked closer to the saddle and I saw more of the avalanche chute, which was covered in huckleberry bushes, I remarked, "This looks like a great place for grizzlies." Immediately after I uttered the words, I looked at the other side of the saddle. About 30 yards in front of us was a female grizzly and her yearling cub busily eating huckleberries.

I was in the lead as we approached the saddle. I already had my bear spray out because of the awesome habitat unfolding in front of us. Upon seeing the bears, we immediately froze and began whispering about a possible strategy. We obviously did not want to alert the bears to our presence. We felt we were entirely too close. Jim suggested we turn around and head back the way we came, but I did not want to lose sight of the bears. I felt if we turned around and she suddenly became aware of our presence, she could run into us with very little warning. We talked about other possibilities when all of a sudden, she stood up, looked in our direction, and put her nose in the air. A photo at that time would have been incredible. However, we could not even consider taking that chance.

The bear could not see us even though we were fairly close. We were hiding behind tree branches right at the saddle and she was looking towards the sun. All of a sudden, she fell down on all fours and took off like a bolt of lightning. With her cub right behind, she crashed down the avalanche chute away from us. We pressed forward to watch. It was then that we saw a second cub following her.

I feel the strategy of not wanting to lose sight of the bears was correct. I thought we were too close to turn our backs on those bears. Obviously, we were in a tight spot, and if we had made any noise, a charge was a distinct possibility. She reacted to our scent and as often occurs in the vast majority of cases; she ran in the opposite direction.

Glacier National Park, August, 2004

I was hiking along a trail in the late afternoon when I ran into a group of people watching a mother grizzly and two yearling cubs eating serviceberries about 150 yards above the trail. They said that another family group consisting of a mother and two cubs-of-the-year had just crossed the trail and were now in thick cover below us. Since I was interested in observing this particular family group, I decided to hike up the trail to see if I could see them from a better angle. I also figured that the mother and two yearlings would be out for a while and if I could not find the mother with cubs-of-the-year, I could come back and watch this family.

I proceeded up the trail. I scanned the area thoroughly without any results. There was no sign of the younger family group. After 20 minutes I turned around and headed back to the group of people and the older bear family. Much to my surprise, when I rounded the corner where they had been, there were no people and no bears. The only thing I could deduce was that the older family group dropped down the hillside, crossed the trail, and disappeared into the thick cover.

I now retraced my steps up the trail to see if I could find this older family group. I scanned the same area as before and still saw nothing. I decided to sit down on a large rock next to the trail and listen for anything moving in the heavy cover below the trail. I soon heard brush moving about 80 yards below and to the left of my position. At first, I thought it was either the older family group or a moose, because I had seen many moose in this same area.

Just then a bear came into view (Photo 25). Then another bear popped into view. I was totally surprised! It was the mother and two cubs-of-the-year! They had probably been in the area the whole time I was hiking back and forth on the trail.

Photo 25

The female started moving towards the trail with the two youngsters close behind. She looked right at me but showed no sign of concern with my presence. Since I was still, calm, and very visible (I was now standing on the trail), I expected this reaction. Since I had a good view of her and her cubs, I did not want to change my position. Either backing up the trail or proceeding down past them would have resulted in my losing sight of them. In addition, any movement by me might have changed her behavior.

I stayed where I was and continued to take photos. As she neared the trail, she stopped periodically and ate serviceberries. Her cubs were curious but not nervous (Photo 26). She crossed the trail right in front of me. When she reached the other side of the trail, she stopped to continue eating berries. She even turned her back to me. This was the

Photo 26

most obvious sign that she did not perceive me as a threat. The bears continued moving up the mountainside until they disappeared from view.

My years of experience have taught me that keeping my eyes on the bear(s) and remaining still and calm is one of the most effective strategies for encountering bears. This incident is a prime example of the strategy's success. Quick movements and/or yelling and screaming might have alarmed the bear and produced the opposite results. Once again, seeing how a bear reacts to your presence before you act will usually determine how to correctly act.

Glacier National Park, August, 2005

It was late morning on a hot August day when I started my second hike. I had already been up one trail earlier without

Photo 27

seeing any grizzlies. I started up this second trail into a decent serviceberry area where I had seen grizzlies before. I hadn't gone far when I spotted a mother grizzly and what appeared to be a two-year-old cub. They were working their way down towards the trail, eating berries along the way. I stopped and watched the bears and took a few photos (Photo 27). As I was standing on the trail more people came up behind me. I told them that if we remain calm and still, we would be okay. No body freaked out.

Farther up the trail other hikers had stopped in a group. Nobody was doing anything to agitate this bear family. There was plenty of space between our two groups for the bears to cross the trail, if they so desired. As the bears approached the trail, a person in the other group started yelling at us to back up. This was not a good idea because there was a large group of trees

Photo 28

right behind us. If we backed up, we would lose sight of these grizzlies which would not be smart. We remained calm and still with the grizzlies in plain sight. Nobody was uncomfortable with the situation, including the bears. My bear spray was readily available, but I saw no reason to take it out.

The person who just yelled at us yelled again saying he was a volunteer Park person and for us to back up. We ignored him because it was not safe to do so. I saw him reach for his radio and apparently call in this activity. The mother grizzly came down to the trail first (Photo 28). She crossed the trail and began eating more berries (Photo 29). You can see the other group in the background. The only person that could possibly agitate the bears was the volunteer yelling. The cub soon came down to the trail not far behind the mother (Photo 30). In Photo 31 it appears

Photo 29

Photo 30

Photo 31

Photo 32

to be coming right at us, but is actually just catching up to its mother (Photo 32). It should be noted that all photos were taken at 13x magnification.

The bears were calmly eaten berries when a "bear" ranger suddenly came up behind us. He got in front of us, stopped, took off his backpack, and proceeded to pull out a large 44 magnum revolver. The calm tone of the group I was with immediately became one of extreme concern. You could cut the tension with a knife. The bears behavior did not change at all. After the ranger pulled out the gun, he ordered us back into the trees and he followed. The result was we could no longer see the grizzlies. By this time the bears could be 10 yards from us, and we would not be able to see them because the trees were so thick. The group of people up the trail from us could not see the bears (I assumed) because of the thick berry bushes between them and the bears. We were not in what I would call a good situation.

After a few minutes I volunteered to go down the trail to the other side of the trees where it was more open so I could hopefully see where the bears were. At this time, I took out my bear spray, took the safety off and started making noise so the bears, if they were still around, would know where I was. As I got around the trees, I could see the two grizzlies heading downhill, away from the trail into thick cover. I let the others know and left and started back down the trail to the trailhead. I made noise all the way back and kept my bear spray out.

CHAPTER 7

HIKING ALONE

Hiking alone is not the recommended way of traveling. However, it can be extremely rewarding if you can do it in a safe manner. Hiking alone is rife with potential hazards and risks. Two of the biggest risks anywhere, not just in grizzly country, are getting lost and getting injured. Also, in grizzly country, there is no one to help you make noise or look for bears. The exception might be a popular trail that gets a lot of hiking traffic. Do not count on a cell phone to call for help. Much of grizzly country has no cell phone service. If you have a problem with a grizzly, you could be on your own. However, even with all these risks, hiking alone can be rewarding if you do it in a safe manner.

I hike alone. I will hike with others whenever possible, but since I hike almost every day, when most normal people are working, I often end up going alone. I do not consider this dangerous because I follow safe hiking practices. When you hike alone you must pay attention, think about what you are doing, and make more noise. You have to stay focused. As a result of hiking alone, I have seen many incredible things that I may not have seen had I been in a group of hikers. The following situations shed some light on the risks and rewards of hiking alone.

Yellowstone National Park - June 2008

It was the middle of elk calving season in Yellowstone. I started on the trail at about 7:30 am, hiking to an open ridge where cow elk had been seen. About half way up in a small open area between two groups of trees I caught a flash of something brown moving down the sagebrush hillside about 150 yards ahead of me. It was a small elk calf running down the hill with a grizzly in hot pursuit with the mother elk and a coyote on the heels of the bear. This was amazing. I have witnessed both grizzlies and black bears killing elk calves, but only from the road.

The grizzly caught the calf in a second. Death was instant. I watched intently as the cow elk and coyote circled the bear. The grizzly was already beginning to tear into the calf. It was then that I decided to take my camera out and start taking photos. The bear had looked at me; it was aware of my presence. The distance between us was great enough that I believed it did not consider me a threat. Soon the bear's nose was red with blood (Photo 33). After a few minutes I wanted to continue my hike, but the trail went closer to the bear. I did not want to get any closer, so I decided to bushwhack around the grizzly. I was slightly downhill from the bear. As I bushwhacked, I gained elevation and soon was above the grizzly. The bear looked up right at me and made a step in my direction. She, whom I later learned was a five-year-old female, was not happy. She probably thought that I was either a threat or I was competing for the calf. I instantly froze and in a calm soothing voice said, "What a good bear, what a pretty bear." She stopped, but kept looking at me. I slowly retreated downhill the exact way I had come up. As I started downhill, she went back to eating. I went back to the area where I had been, and she continued to eat.

Photo 33

After about twenty minutes two hikers came up the trail to me. When the bear now saw three of us, she picked up the dead calf and carried it into a group of trees away from us. There she continued to eat. I felt it was a good time to continue my hike to the open ridge. Once again, I went around her, but was now far enough away that she did not even pay attention. About two hours later I came back the same way. She was just finishing consuming the calf. As I came down, she left the carcass and moved up the ridge where I had just been.

There is one thing I should not have done. I should not have tried to go around her the first time. I felt that I was at a safe distance, but she did not feel the same way. At least I kept my eyes on her in order to watch her reaction to my movements. The second I saw that she may be agitated, I froze. This calmed the bear, and I was able to retreat. In hindsight, I should have remained where I first saw her or should have hiked back down to the trailhead. When hiking alone risks are magnified. The right decisions need to be made.

Glacier National Park - Eastside - June 2010

I started alone down a popular trail at about nine a.m. I passed many hikers and knew there were more ahead of me. As I approached a cliff area, I noticed a small group of people looking up. When I asked them what they were looking at, they pointed into the cliffs at a mother grizzly with three cubs that were born earlier that year (known as cubs-of-the-year). I took out my binoculars and saw three little brown bundles of fur. Mother grizzlies with three cubs of any age are not common in Glacier. I was happy with this sighting. Soon the other people left, and I moved off the trail a bit to get a better angle of view. The bears were about 250 yards above me. I took out my camera and started taking pictures.

The bears were grazing on lush green grass on small flat areas interspersed in the band of cliffs. The mom and two of the cubs went up a large crack in the cliff face. The third cub kept grazing. The little cub finally realized that its mom and siblings were gone when they appeared directly above it on top of the twenty-foot, almost sheer rock face. The baby bear panicked and started climbing straight up. I wish I would have had a video camera. I did not know if the little one could make it, but after a couple of minutes it successfully climbed to the top where the mother grizzly was patiently waiting (Photo 34).

I had never seen anything like this. It was a completely safe situation for anyone watching. If I had refused to hike that day because I was alone, I would have missed this magical event. This mother and her three cubs would be regular visitors on the trails in this area over the next two years. She will be discussed in the chapter "Tolerant Grizzlies." I was lucky to see this family group near the beginning of their lives together.

Photo 34

Glacier National Park - Eastside - Early June 2013

It was about 8 a.m. on a sunny morning. I was driving a road looking for bears. Every now and then I would stop to look at distant open areas with my binoculars. I stopped again to look at an avalanche chute across a large body of water. I had looked at this area many times over the years and had never seen anything. This time, to my surprise, there were two young grizzlies 'play' mating high up in the avalanche chute. It was, after all, mating season. I knew these two bears from seeing them a few times before. They had been together the previous fall and this spring. The female was a three-year-old and had a radio ear tag. We (the people who had previously seen them) figured that the male was either three or four years old. Since a hiking trail crossed the bottom of the chute, I decided to hike the trail to get a better view. The chute was about a mile from the trailhead, and it took me about twenty-five minutes to reach it. I made noise the whole way and hiked with my bear spray out with the safety clip off. The bears would be out of sight until I got within about 100 yards of the chute.

As I got close, I looked up the chute and did not see the bears. Then I looked straight ahead and saw the male on the trail about 60 yards ahead of me. The young female was in the chute about twenty yards above a line of trees. It was then that I heard some twigs snap behind me and to my right. I thought it was the female coming down towards the trail through the trees and heavy brush. As I turned my head towards the sound, I was totally dumbfounded to see a very large dark male grizzly walk right by me 10 feet away. I instinctively froze. What else could I do? Time seemed to stand still. All I could do was stand there with my mouth agape as I followed this large grizzly with my eyes. (Photo 35)

Photo 35

At this point, I had no idea where the young grizzlies went. The 'big boy' had my full attention. This large male ended up in a large, lush meadow right next to the water. I turned around and hiked back to the trailhead. I never saw the young bears again that day. The large dark male bear was known as "Buster." I had seen him earlier that year, but only at a distance. Buster had, without me knowing it, followed me down the trail. I soon realized the implications of what had happened. All my attention had been in front of me. I was not even thinking about behind me. From that day on, I stop much more often and look behind as I hike. Of course, I am not sure what I would have done if I had looked behind me that day. Since I had gotten a good look of him, I estimated his weight at 500 pounds. That means that in the fall he could have been a 700-pound bear - among the largest in the ecosystem. I have always said that large males like to keep track of what is going on in their territory. Most of the time you will never see them. The main exception is during mating season.

This was a very close encounter, one that I would not want to experience again. I was alone. I had my bear spray out, and Buster was only ten feet away. Fortunately, he exhibited no signs of aggression. There was no reason to spray him, and it would have been wrong to do so. Why would I want to aggravate a huge grizzly only ten feet away from me? There are definitely times to use bear spray; this was not one of them. The outcome of this encounter was as good as it could be. I am not sure if hiking with any other people would have changed it. It is possible another member of the party could have panicked. In that type of situation, hiking alone might be preferable. You need to know who you hike with, and they need to know how to react in an encounter. Everyone I hike with knows how to remain calm in encounter situations.

In hindsight, I never should have been on this hike. I broke one of my own safe hiking admonishments: Keep your eye on the bear(s). The minute I left the road, I lost sight of the two young bears. I really had no idea where they would be when I got to the avalanche chute. I was taking an unnecessary risk. One needs to reduce risks in grizzly country, not increase them.

Glacier National Park - October 2014

There was construction underway near a main hotel, so the trailhead I wanted was not accessible by car. I had to hike about two miles around a small lake to reach it. Since I planned to go all the way to the head of a high mountain lake, it would be a sixteen-mile day.

I wanted to get to the lake to see if any grizzlies were eating hedysarum in the large open areas around the powder blue body of water. After reaching the trailhead, I hiked about four miles without incident. As I approached a small bridge crossing a creek, I noticed a young couple with backpacks coming my way. I figured they must have camped overnight at the lake.

I asked them if that was the case. They acknowledged that they had, and that they had seen two grizzlies the evening before, digging. They also stated they had just spooked a grizzly about a half mile further up the trail. It had run uphill into the brush and disappeared. I thanked them for the information and continued up the trail. I noted they both carried bear spray.

I continued my hike knowing there might be as many as three grizzlies, maybe more, in the area. My hiking goal or strategy did not change. I knew that I could encounter grizzlies on any hike I took in the area. A bit further up the trail, as I rounded a corner, I saw a grizzly on the trail about forty yards ahead of me. It was looking directly at me. I froze and watched this bear's reaction. It was calm. I was calm. I softly talked to the bear as I reached for my camera. I took a couple of photos (Photo 36) before the bear turned to my left and disappeared uphill into heavy cover. I waited a minute and then continued hiking. When I reached the lake there were fresh diggings of hedysarum, probably from the previous night, all over the open areas. Some were within one hundred yards of the campground. I glassed the entire area without seeing any more grizzlies. As I hiked back, I thought about a number of things, all the while making appropriate noise. If I had not met the couple, I still would have done the exact same things. I might have been surprised to see the grizzly on the trail, but I would have reacted

Photo 36

the same way. As stated earlier, I knew I had a good chance to see grizzlies on this hike. The hike and encounter also validated my hiking strategy when hiking alone: Make noise and carry bear spray readily accessible. Many times, I carry my spray in hand with the safety clip off. I feel comfortable doing this, but be careful not to spray yourself or anyone else, especially if you trip or fall.

Glacier National Park - Eastside - May 2015

A good friend of mine, wildlife biologist Shane Conner, and I decided to spend a couple of days on the east side of Glacier hiking numerous drainages looking for grizzly diggings, tracks, scat, and other signs, and in the process perhaps seeing a grizzly.

We took one trail to get above the valley floor. We glassed the entire area without spotting anything and started hiking back. About half way down we hit a trail junction. Since we wanted to cover as much of the area as possible, we decided to take a different way back. As we reached a lake, we noticed that the footbridge across a decent-sized creek had not been installed for the season. We did not want to wade the creek, so we turned back.

We had passed a horse trail before we came to the creek. As we came to it again, we decided to hike back on it. It soon became quite muddy with much standing water. Shane decided to turn back. I decided to keep going. We would meet each other at our vehicles, if not sooner on the trail.

As I continued down the horse trail, I started to notice fairly fresh grizzly tracks coming from the opposite direction. They appeared to be those of a large male, maybe Buster. I kept going. I was making noise and of course, had my bear spray out. I was now, after all, hiking alone. A little bit further I came around a corner and there was a grizzly on the trail about 25 yards in front of me. It had heard me coming and was looking right at me. The scene was eerily similar to the one I had experienced the previous fall (see above).

Once again, I froze. This time, however, the bear did not seem calm. At first, I thought it might be a small adult female with a cub, but I could not see much behind the bear because of heavy brush. I soon realized it was a lone young bear. I was thinking about getting out my camera, but the bear started to move its lower jaw up and down. This was not necessarily a sign of aggression, but it was at least a sign of agitation. I forgot about taking pictures. I started to talk to the bear in soft tones, "Oh, what a good bear. . . oh, what a pretty bear." The bear seemed to relax. It walked off the trail and slowly made its way around me.

As soon as the bear was about 50 yards to my right, I

continued down the trail, keeping my eye on it and continuing to talk in a soft and calm manner until the bear was out of sight. As I hiked, I noticed the bear's tracks in the mud. They appeared to be the size of a two-year-old bear. When I reached the main hiking trail a few minutes later, I followed them to the east. The young grizzly's tracks had originated about a mile further down. Bears use hiking trails.

I finally met Shane at the parking lot. We talked about what had happened. We agreed that taking a picture in my situation was not worth the risk. Making noise, having bear spray, and being able to freeze and remain calm when the situation calls for it, are three of the basic tenets of hiking safely in grizzly country, whether you are alone or not.

If you hike alone, let someone know where you are going and when you will be back. Leave a note on your car if you need to. If you are afraid of grizzlies or you can not adhere to safe hiking strategies, do not hike alone in grizzly country.

Glacier National Park - Late September 2017

I started hiking about 8 am. It was clear and calm. My main objective for the day was to reach a high mountain pass about 4.5 miles ahead. It was a good area for hedysarum, a prime food source for grizzlies this time of year. As I hiked, I was in the shadow of a large mountain just to the east. The sun was just coming up and I was eager to break into good light.

I broke into an open area about one-and-a-half hours later. I could see the pass, which was now bathed in sunshine. As I continued, I looked for signs of digging and, of course, for bears. I saw neither. I had my bear spray out and was making noise. I reached the pass at about 10:15. I glassed in all directions without any luck. There still was no sign of any diggings. I decided to keep hiking over the pass to where

I could see an open valley to the west and north. I soon ran into deep snow on the trail that had drifted in. I decided to cross a small scree field to the edge of a cliff to get a better view without losing elevation. When I got to the edge of the cliff, I looked straight down to the trail below. Much to my surprise, I saw an adult grizzly right below me on the trail, walking towards the pass, where I had just been. Because of the switchbacks on that side of the pass, the bear was actually walking away from me. Once it hit the last switchback, it would be walking towards me.

I had a quick decision to make. I could either stay where I was and risk getting stuck on the west side of the pass and possibly the cliff itself, or I could scramble back across the scree field to the pass before the grizzly reached it. I chose to do the latter. I was able to keep my eye on the bear the whole way. The bear was not yet in the sun, but it would be once it was near the pass.

I reached the pass and was a safe distance from the bear, which was walking rather slowly. It also had farther to go because it remained on the trail. After the grizzly passed the last switchback, the sun started to hit it. I pulled my camera out from its hip pack and started to take pictures (Photo 37, Photo 38). I was directly on top of the pass. The bear appeared to not be aware of my presence. The sun was right behind my back, and it was calm. I did not believe the bear could smell me or see me because when it looked up it was looking right into the sun.

As the bear moved closer, I backed down the trail and stopped. I continued to take photos as the grizzly approached the top of the pass (Photo 39). It was then, I believe, the bear picked up my scent from where I had just been standing on the trail at the top of the pass, because the grizzly immediately

Photo 37

moved off the trail to the south. I continued watching the bear until it stopped about 300 yards away and looked directly at me. The bear was now in a position where the sun was no longer in its eyes. I continued to watch the bear for about a half hour while it meandered in the scree and crossed snowfields. It appeared to be searching for hedysarum, but I never saw it digging. I decided to leave and head back to the trailhead. I felt incredibly blessed for this very rare sighting.

I thought about my actions during this "encounter" when I got back to my vehicle. As I had approached the cliff, I was making noise, but because of the rock face directly above the grizzly, I do not believe it heard me. Once I spotted the grizzly on the trail below, I quit making noises until I started back to the trailhead. There was no need to spook this bear. It was a safe distance away and I had clear views all around. The

Photo 38

whole time I watched and photographed this bear there was no indication that it was stressed and most of the time acted as if it had no idea I was there, although I will never know that for sure. My bear spray was always readily available on

Photo 39

my hip holsters if I did not have one already in hand. Once I left the bear near the pass, I made noise and continued to carry my bear spray out until I reached the trailhead. In other words, I followed my regular hiking strategy for hiking alone. It should also be noted that I never saw another hiker until I was on my way back.

In October 2015 I started to carry a Personal Locator Beacon, PLB for short. This device (which I had on this hike) can be used to either send a pre-programmed message to someone (my wife, for example) or send an S.O.S.. I have mine set up to send a preset message to my wife through email stating that everything is fine. This way I can send a reassuring message when I am out of cell phone range for a long time. The S.O.S. message is sent to an organization specially dedicated to alerting the proper authorities. It is to be used only in life threatening situations. Both messages are sent through satellites that automatically record your exact location. The use of this device requires an annual subscription. Like bear spray, I feel it is better to have it and not need it than to need it and not have it. Hopefully, I will never have to use the S.O.S. message. In any case, it provides a special means of communication, especially when hiking alone and/or bushwhacking.

CHAPTER 8
BUSHWHACKING

Bushwhacking refers to hiking "off trail." This is not a recommended way of travel in any situation let alone in grizzly country. Footing can be difficult and dangerous. Hazards can be difficult to see or even completely hidden. Downfall (downed trees), slippery rocks and logs, holes, dips, cliffs, water hazards, heavy brush, etc. can make hiking not only extremely difficult, but also very dangerous. If anything happens, getting help can be problematical at best.

When you throw in the presence of grizzly bears, the potential for negative outcomes increases. Therefore, risk-reward analyses need to be seriously made. I have been to incredible places that could only be reached by bushwhacking. On some of these travels I have also run into dangerous situations. The following experiences illustrate some of the many dangers one could encounter while bushwhacking.

Yellowstone National Park - Early May, 2007

Jim Cole and I had been driving the park roads while we were waited for the arrival of Sabrina Leigh, a young lady who had recently become interested in the ecology of grizzly bears. It was Sabrina's first visit to Yellowstone, and we wanted her to be able to safely observe her first Yellowstone grizzlies. After overcoming some serious car problems, Sabrina finally arrived. The road scenario was not turning out to be very productive. We decided to take a hike in Hayden Valley. Even though we would be bushwhacking, we felt that the open vistas of the valley offered the best chances of seeing a grizzly at a safe distance.

From the road, Hayden Valley looks like it would be an easy place to hike and spot bears. However, as stated in previous chapters, looks can be deceiving. Hayden Valley is primarily a sagebrush landscape containing many small dips, knolls, ridges, low hills, and islands of trees. It is imperative that one make noise and have bear spray readily accessible. Jim and I had hiked this particular section of the valley many times. We were well aware of the risks and related these to Sabrina before we started. Sabrina was an experienced hiker, but she was new to Yellowstone.

We started our hike at about 2:30 in the afternoon from a pullout along the road. We were taking the easiest route we knew. It also afforded the best views without venturing more than a mile from the road on a four-mile, cross-country loop. In addition to grizzlies one of the unique things about Yellowstone are the many thermal features. Our planned route would basically circle around some of these very interesting - and possibly dangerous - formations. Another thing that makes Yellowstone different from any other national park are the herds of free-roaming bison. Most people don't realize how huge and fast these animals are. As a matter of fact, I am more concerned with running into bison at close range than a grizzly. We were all on constant alert for the many possible hazards we could encounter.

We were about 2.5 miles into our hike, going around some thermal features. We were making appropriate noise. We were all carrying bear spray. Jim was in the lead when he suddenly blurted, "There's a grizzly!" I looked up and saw the bear about 150 yards in front of us. We stopped, stood still, and watched the young bear. The grizzly stopped and watched us. The grizzly was fairly easy to spot because (1) it was on top of a small ridge and (2) the sagebrush was only about a foot high. (Photo 40) Different terrain characteristics, such as higher sagebrush, could have made the grizzly much harder, or even impossible to see.

After watching us for a moment, the grizzly ambled to the north and disappeared over the ridge. We continued our hike on the planned route without seeing any more bears and without further incident. We had followed safe hiking procedures even though we were still bushwhacking. We were all glad that we were able to safely see this bear. It definitely made the hike worthwhile.

Photo 40

Glacier National Park - August, 2007

My sister, Debby Nelson, had been working at one of the park hotels for a good portion of the summer. She was fortunate to have hiked many of the trails near the hotel. She was also fortunate to have observed many grizzlies On this particular day we decided to do a hike I had done a few times before. A good portion of this 12-mile hike would involve bushwhacking, including some cliff climbing. Debby was more than willing to attempt this endeavor, because of the special opportunities it offered for viewing wildlife, especially grizzlies.

We started hiking about 7 a.m. It had been a dry summer and several large wildfires were burning in northwest Montana. The rising sun produced a reddish hue in the smokey air. After about a mile and a half on a well-traveled trail, we started hiking upwards on an old game trail. We soon encountered heavy brush and thick forest. Huckleberry bushes with ripe berries were interspersed throughout the area. Making noise was essential. We both had bear spray. I had one can in my hand with the safety off.

The going was slow because of the limited visibility and steep, rough terrain. After about 20-30 minutes we broke into an area below a band of reddish cliffs. I looked up and much to my surprise and delight I immediately saw a mother grizzly and a yearling cub on top of one of the rock outcrops, studying us. She no doubt heard us coming. We froze and watched her reaction to us, which was basically the same as our reaction to her. After realizing we were not a threat to them, they started to move down towards an area of small trees surrounded by huckleberry bushes. We remained still and watched them. The bears soon disappeared into the thick cover.

We now faced a dilemma. The game trail went into the thick brush the grizzlies had just entered. There was no way we were going there. We talked about our options. We decided to detour up and around. Because of the abundance of huckleberries, we figured the grizzly family was partaking of the delicious fruit. We basically headed up to where bears had been when we first saw them. The hillside there was quite open and offered us a direct line of sight into the cover where the grizzlies had disappeared.

We continued to make noise as we circled the area. I could now see where the game trail continued on the other side of the thick cover. We had to go slightly downhill and cross a small ravine to get back on the game trail. As I crossed the ravine, I looked down and was slightly surprised to see the mother grizzly and her cub taking a refreshing dip in a small pool of water.

Once more we froze, remained calm, and watched how the grizzlies reacted to our presence. Once again, the mother showed no sign of agitation. I took out my camera and took some photos (Photos 41 and 42). In Photo 42 the mother looks like she may be roaring. Actually, she is yawning. The cub moved out of view while the mother grizzly laid back down in the small pool. Debby and I slowly continued our climb, all the while making noise (there could have been other bears in the area) and keeping an eye on the two bears now well below us. The mother eventually got out of the water and followed her cub into the huckleberry bushes.

We continued our hike without further incident. Once again, the sighting of grizzlies made it an exceptional experience. I believed we followed safe hiking procedures, except for the fact that we were bushwhacking. The most dangerous portion of the bushwhacking was climbing some cliffs we encountered after we left the grizzlies. Making noise, carrying bear spray, and knowing how to react when a grizzly

Photo 41

is encountered can lessen the risks of bushwhacking, but cannot eliminate them.

Photo 42

BUSHWHACKING GONE WRONG

Hayden Valley, Yellowstone National Park - May 23, 2007

I knew Jim Cole was in Yellowstone. I had talked to him the previous day. I had just spent the night up the North Fork of the Flathead River across from the western boundary of Glacier National Park. I started hiking up a gated road in the Whitefish Mountain Range west of the river at about 7:30 a.m. I was hiking alone so I had my bear spray out with the safety off and I was making noise. My destination was some avalanche chutes about 7.5 miles up the road where I hoped to catch a glimpse of a grizzly. Unbeknownst to me, Jim Cole, at about 8:30 a.m. would begin a bushwhack through Hayden Valley, also hoping to get a glimpse of a grizzly.

As I neared my destination, I studied the large avalanche chutes on the north side of the road. It was a beautiful, clear day so I had good visibility all the way to the top of the ridge where the chutes originated. After a few minutes of glassing, I continued up the road. A few minutes later I heard and saw an airplane circling above the avalanche chutes I had just been looking at. I reversed direction and went toward the slide areas. The plane soon left, but it had piqued my curiosity. It had been my experience that circling planes in remote areas usually indicates some sort of wildlife study, survey, or actual sighting. Considering the area, I felt a radio-collared grizzly could have been the object of the planes' attention.

I again reached the bottom of the chutes, looked up with my binoculars, and immediately saw a grizzly about 800 yards away in some thick brush that had not yet leafed out. It was about 10 a.m. I soon saw another grizzly, then another. It was a radio collared mother with a pair of 2 two-year-old cubs. I observed them for another 30 minutes. I even saw them nurse, after which they moved into thick cover and disappeared. I headed home. It had been a very rewarding hike. I got home about 4 p.m., related the details of my trip to my wife, had dinner, took a shower, and went to bed.

About 3 a.m. we were awakened by the phone ringing.

As probably with most people, a call in the middle of the night, was a very rare occurrence. I jumped out of bed and answered the phone. It was a good friend of Jim's who lived in Colorado. I knew something bad had happened. The friend said Jim had been severely mauled by a grizzly the previous morning (while I was hiking in the Whitefish Range). He was now in a hospital in Idaho Falls. I did not go back to bed. Suzi got up and made coffee.

A few hours later I started to make phone calls. I needed to let friends know what happened, and I wanted to find out if there was any information about the attack. There were scattered reports on the internet, but the stories were just rumor or conjecture. Most of the people I talked to could not believe Jim got mauled again. Has anyone ever been mauled twice by grizzly bears?

I started to get first hand reports of Jim's condition. A friend at the hospital said Jim was heavily sedated after undergoing many hours of surgery to reconstruct his face, which had been almost completely torn off. Jim's friend did not know any details of the attack. Only later on Saturday, May 26, when Jim called after regaining suitable consciousness, would I begin to learn what happened.

Jim said that he started bushwhacking through Hayden Valley at about 8:30 am. He told me his route, which we had done together numerous times. He said that he had just started on his way back to the road when he dropped over a small knoll and caught a dark flash out of the corner of his eye. It was coming towards him. The grizzly drove him into the ground. He had no chance to grab his bear spray which was on his pack belt on his waist. This sounded eerily like his first mauling.

Jim tried to grab his spray, but he was face down on the

ground with the grizzly on top of him, pinning him down. Jim could not move his right arm. The grizzly took its left paw, slid it under Jim's head, and with one motion tore the upper portion of his face towards the left. Jim did not know this at the time. He just remembered that all of a sudden the grizzly was not on top of him any longer. He glanced up to see a blurry image of a mother grizzly and at least one cub-of-the-year running away.

Jim realized that he had to get out of there ASAP! He knew his legs worked. However, he was bleeding profusely from his face and about the only thing he could see was the sun, through a slit in his right eyelid when he bent his head back. Because he knew the area so well, he knew the fastest way back to the road would be along and through Trout Creek. It would not be easy, but it was his best chance of survival. Luckily, he made it to the road at a pullout where the road crosses the creek. Visitors who had been enjoying the vista of Hayden Valley immediately attended to him. Help was soon on its way. He was transported to West Yellowstone by ambulance and from there airlifted by helicopter to the hospital in Idaho Falls.

It took a long time for Jim to recover. He lost all vision in his left eye. His face, although reconstructed, looked very deformed. Although he could hike and drive and otherwise live a "normal" life, he suffered pain and problems for the next three years. Jim died of natural causes in July 2010.

I never met another person with as much passion for, and dedication to the preservation of, the grizzly. Each year we hiked not scores or hundreds of miles together, but thousands. We not only looked for grizzlies, but we sought out as much knowledge as we could through direct observation of their habitat. I wish he were still with us. I miss him greatly.

In looking back at Jim's second mauling, a few factors stick out. First, Jim was hiking alone. Second, he was bushwhacking. Nobody knew where he was. His vehicle was parked at a pullout, but that was a common sight. Nobody would have had any indication of any problem until it got dark, and his vehicle was still there, or most likely not until the next morning. Third, and most importantly, Jim said he was not making any noise. The lack of noise resulted in the dangerous closeness of the surprise encounter.

Jim was carrying two cans of bear spray on his pack's waistbelt, but because of the close proximity of the bear and the speed of its attack, there was no time to draw a can from its holster, much less flip off the safety and release the spray. I don't know if the attack could have been prevented if Jim had been carrying a can of bear spray in his hand with the safety off, but I believe it would not have hurt. Would a burst of spray even as the bear hit him have lessened the severity of the attack? I don't know. It's easy to be a "Monday morning quarterback," but in grizzly country, one's focus must always be safe hiking protocol. As noted earlier, because of what I witnessed during Jim's first marling almost 14 years earlier, I now carry a can of bear spray ***in my hand with the safety off*** a good deal of the time, especially when hiking alone and/or bushwhacking.

I think about what happened to Jim a lot. I think about my own adventures bushwhacking alone. I have had a few rewarding bushwhacks, but mostly, the rewards were definitely not worth the risks. Bushwhacking, especially alone, can turn into a very dangerous endeavor.

CHAPTER NINE

CAMPING IN GRIZZLY COUNTRY

Sometimes when I hike in grizzly country, I will spend one or more nights in order to cover the areas I want to observe. This involves both frontcountry and backcountry stays. I define frountcountry camping as any campsite accessible by vehicle. Backcountry sites can only be accessed on foot, horse, watercraft, or aircraft. The most important aspect of either experience is proper food storage so bears are not attracted to your campsite. This sounds obvious, but many people have no clue that leaving out food, including garbage, or improperly storing it can—and probably will—cause problems. A grizzly that becomes food conditioned, that is, that has learned to seek food and garbage from people and from places where people are, usually ends up dead. Also, bears can become emboldened in such situations and attack people in order to get food.

When camping in the frontcountry, your vehicle is usually the best place to store food. Garbage should be stored just like food and packed out just like food. To a bear our garbage is food. Some frontcountry campsites, especially in national parks, offer bear proof food storage cabinets. Some backcountry sites also offer such containers. Frontcountry campgrounds usually have bear-resistant garbage cans. In any case, any attractant (anything that has an odor), including food, garbage, drinks, toothpaste, and other toiletries, must be properly stored away from bears.

Backcountry camping offers unique challenges for food handling and storage. When I reach the campsite, I immediately secure my food, then I set up my tent. All designated backcountry campsites in national parks I have visited have some way to store food out of the reach of bears. These include vertical food poles, high cables strung up parallel to the ground, or a metal pipe set up parallel to the ground. The vertical poles have hooks welded near the top. You use a long pole (supplied at the camping area) to transfer your food bag up onto one of a few hooks at the top of the stationary food pole. I personally do not like this setup. If your food bag does not have a metal ring or carabineer at the end of it, it becomes quite difficult to hang your bag on a high hook, especially in low light. I much prefer the cable or simple horizontal pipe (Photo 43). You tie a weight (like a rock or stick) to one end of a long (20-25 foot), small diameter rope such as a parachute cord. Throw the weighted end over the cable or pipe, tie the other end to your food bag and hoist it up. Then untie the weight and tie off that end to the vertical poles on either side. Under any system the goal is to get your food bag at least 10 feet off the ground.

In undesignated campsites, such as those in wilderness areas or off trail, you must find a tree with a suitable, high branch to hang your food bag. It should be 10 feet or more off the ground and several feet from the tree trunk. If you are in a treeless area, such as tundra or at high elevations, the best solution is a bear proof "food barrel." I have used these in both situations. The only downside is that such barrels are rather cumbersome to pack.

Photo 43

No matter what system or method is used, the food must be stored as far from your tent as practical. Such distance is usually at least 100 feet and in the case of the barrel on the ground, 100 yards minimum is recommended.

When cooking, a minimum safe distance of at least 100 feet from your tent is also recommended. At designated campsites a food prep area is already constructed and its use is mandatory for cooking and eating. When I am camping by myself in the backcountry, I never cook. I utilize only dry food that needs no preparation to eat. This not only cuts down on packed weight because I need no stove or eating utensils, but it lessens odors that might attract bears.

I have had to camp in areas where I have seen grizzlies near the campground. If this is particularly worrisome, there are portable, battery-powered electric fences available that are made to place around your tent and/or food. They are rather bulky and add weight for backpacking, but if you are backpacking with a group, or are on a pack trip with horses, or are flown in (such as Alaska), the extra weight could provide peace of mind. In Katmai National Park, the only designated campground (that I am aware of) is completely surrounded by an electric fence. In addition, covered food prep areas, secured gear and food/garbage sheds, and running water are provided within the perimeter of the fence.

No matter where I camp, I always take my two cans of bear spray into my tent. One goes in my sleeping bag and the other is on the floor of the tent right next to me. You should also have a bright flashlight and/or headlamp at hand.

The best thing to do for camping, either in the frontcountry or backcountry, is proper preparation. This includes preparing for any weather related problems, having enough food and water or access to a good water supply, a good map, a compass, and letting someone know where and what you are doing. Running into a grizzly is usually the least of my concerns, even though I am thoroughly prepared for such an event. Far more people have been killed from slipping on wet rocks, drowning, falling, getting caught in an avalanche, or hypothermia, than by grizzlies. I believe you have a greater chance of getting killed in an auto accident on your way to the campground or trailhead than from a bear.

CHAPTER TEN

TOLERANT GRIZZLIES

Most of the grizzlies people see or encounter are what I refer to as "tolerant grizzlies." In the past I referred to such grizzlies as "habituated," but I feel that this term, as used by most people, is derogatory. It implies that grizzlies may lose their "natural fear" of humans after repeated exposure to us. I am not convinced that grizzlies have a natural "fear" of us. Instead, I believe in many cases that grizzlies have a natural

Photo 44

"toleration" of humans. Nevertheless, whether fearful or tolerant, ***no grizzly likes being surprised at close range—by anything.***

Grizzlies can be tolerant in one situation and wary in another. For example, the Yellowstone grizzly known as "264" (Photo 44) was incredibly tolerant near the road with her cubs. In the backcountry, with her cubs, you would swear she was a different bear. However, there are reasons why grizzlies may behave differently in such situations. After years of observation, I have learned many things about these, usually, very tolerant animals.

THE BEGINNING OF UNDERSTANDING

Denali National Park, July and August, 1994

Jim Cole and I did volunteer work for the United States Biological Survey (a temporary offshoot of the United States Geological Survey, also known as the USGS) in Alaska's Denali National Park in the summer of 1994. Jim basically spent the whole summer there. I did not arrive until the middle of July and spent about three weeks there. Our "job" was to find and observe as many grizzlies as possible. It was like we were in heaven.

My first few days there involved driving the road to search for grizzlies. It was not difficult. On my first full day we observed 10 grizzlies! I was blown away. I had never seen that many grizzlies from any road, anywhere. We continued this routine for about 10 days. We took some short hikes during that time, but we did not see any bears in the backcountry. All of our observations were from the road. We decided that we needed some backcountry data, so we took a backcountry trip and set up a basecamp on the north-side of Denali, formerly Mount McKinley (Photo 45).

Photo 45

The first morning I looked to the east along the ridge we were camped on and noticed a mother grizzly and one cub-of-the-year moving toward us. She quickly moved over the top of the ridge and out of sight. I don't know if she saw us or picked up our scent, but she was gone. We quickly gathered our radio telemetry equipment and started scanning frequencies, but did not pick up any signals.

We spent the next five days hiking the tundra, mostly along tops of ridges. We would stop and use our telemetry equipment to look for radio-collared grizzlies. During that time, we picked up two different signals, but were never able to actually spot the bears. The tundra turned out to be as deceiving as the sagebrush areas of Yellowstone.

On the mornings of our last two full days, we spotted bears

with our binoculars from our basecamp. The first morning, I spotted what appeared to be two siblings or a mother grizzly and large cub. With our telemetry equipment we discovered that one of the bears was radio-collared. With that information we deduced that the two grizzlies were indeed siblings. The next morning, I spotted a grizzly about 3 miles away. Once again, we used the radio telemetry to discover that this was a radio-collared grizzly, and it was a 23-year-old male!

Jim and I discussed our experience on the way back to where we started our adventure. First, we were amazed that every bear we saw in the backcountry was seen without the aid of our radio equipment. The telemetry only aided in identification, not in finding the bears. Second, we only saw five grizzlies the entire trip, and that included extensive hiking and the use of all the tools at our disposal. Third, finding grizzlies in the road corridor was far more successful than our substantial endeavor in the backcountry. This was exactly the opposite of our expectations. What could possibly be the reason?

Jim pointed out that the only large male we had seen the entire time in the park was in the backcountry. In the road corridor all we saw was mother grizzlies and cubs or lone subadult bears or siblings. Jim came up with the hypothesis that the bears we saw along the road were there because the road and its human activity provided security from large, dominant males, which sometimes kill cubs and chase away subordinate animals. The food sources were almost identical in the road corridor and in the backcountry.

This was a new way of thinking for us. We now had a base of knowledge to work from for what we were about to see in the next couple of decades in the Lower 48.

GLACIER NATIONAL PARK, 2010 & 2011

Orange Sunshine—a very tolerant mother bear

Jim and I started seeing grizzlies near trails and roads on a consistent basis starting in 1997. In Glacier this coincided with one of the best huckleberry years we had ever seen. However, the grizzlies we were seeing were not along the roads, as was beginning to happen in Yellowstone, but rather they were along or even on the hiking trails. At first this concerned us as we had heard about "habituated" bears and believed this was abnormal.

Over the next few years, we realized that this behavior appeared very normal, based on a couple of factors. First, many of the trails (and some of the campgrounds) were built through some of the best berry patches in the ecosystem. Do we really expect grizzlies to forgo these essential food areas simply because people also utilize these areas? Secondly, because many of these same trails are heavily travelled by people, some grizzlies prefer these areas for security reasons just as we saw in Denali. Along heavily travelled hiking trails, as along roads, there appears to be a substantial lack of large dominant males, which younger bears and mothers with cubs try to avoid like the plague. For their part, large males seem to try to avoid people (except, maybe, during mating season) like the plague—perhaps that's how they grow old enough to be large.

So, for less dominant bears and family groups, being near people and away from large males makes sense in terms of survival. One such family was led by a mother grizzly I called "Orange Sunshine" because of the color of her coat. I described the first time I saw them in the chapter "Hiking Alone." They were the bear family where one cub got separated and had to climb a cliff to reach its mother. The second time I saw them was about two weeks later, below a heavily used trail near a lake. It was about 8:30 on a clear sunny morning. The mother was digging glacier lily roots while the still small cubs milled about her and investigated the churned-up soil. I could never get all three in the same frame because they wouldn't't stay still long enough—typical little bears. I'm quite sure the mother bear knew I was in the area because of the noise I had been making. Also, I made no attempt to hide. I remained on or above the trail and did not attempt to get any closer. I was the only person there. I watched them for about an hour before they disappeared from view. I continued to the lake. On my return trip to the trailhead, I saw no sign of them, although I was pretty sure they were still in the area.

After observing them for this second time and this close to the trail, I was leaning towards the idea that she was a fairly tolerant bear. Because of my great respect for these magnificent animals, I felt I needed more observations of this family group before I could confirm my hypothesis. This process would begin to happen in about a month on my very next trip to this part of the park.

I hiked the same trail in the early afternoon of August 10. I had not hiked very far when I saw the same mother and her 3 cubs high above the trail. They were there for ripe serviceberries. As I stood on the trail, the family of grizzlies started moving downhill towards the trail, eating berries as they moved closer. After about an hour, they were right next to the trail and even moved onto it (Photo 46).

By this time a few other people were also watching the bears. However, everyone remained calm and made no sudden movements. The mother grizzly also remained calm and hardly ever looked directly at us. She basically acted as if we were not there, but I am sure she was aware of what we were doing. The cubs, as might be expected, showed signs

Photo 46

Photo 47

of curiosity (Photo 47), but most of the time also seemed to ignore us. Overall, the entire family group was extremely tolerant of our presence.

A couple of weeks later I hiked the same trail. Once again, I saw this same family group in almost the same place above the trail. As before, the mother grizzly and her cubs-of-the-year slowly moved towards the trail as they devoured the ripe serviceberries. The cubs ended up on the trail and two of them started to play at intimidating each other. There were many more people in the area. This didn't seem to affect the bears' actions at all. After milling around the trail for a few minutes (Photo 48), the family was on the move. They proceeded down the trail straight towards a group of people (Photo 49). The people moved out of the way and the grizzlies soon disappeared down a closed portion of an adjoining trail.

The next day a small group of us hiked up the same trail. It was about 11:30 in the morning. The bears were almost in the same place above the trail. This was beginning to look like a favorite spot for the family. It made sense because the serviceberries were some of the best in the ecosystem. This time the grizzly family came down towards the trail a little faster. They were still eating berries, but it seemed that they had somewhere else to go. While the mother ate berries above the trail the cubs came down onto the trail to check us out. The whole family group then disappeared below the trail into thick cover.

Over the years I had seen many grizzlies, both singles and family groups, on or near this trail, but none of them ever came close to epitomizing tolerance as well as this very cohesive family group. In the two-month period since I had first seen them, all the bears were progressing in size and health. I attribute their growth to the incredible food

Photo 48

source which happened to be bisected by the trail. Because of the heavy human traffic on this route, these bears had to be tolerant in order to fully take advantage of the food source and to benefit from the security from large males that the

Photo 49

number of people afforded them. This mother grizzly was doing an outstanding job of successfully raising three cubs.

By the beginning of October, the berries were pretty well gone, except for kinnikinnick. The best kinnikinnick areas were close to the road. I had never seen this family near the road, but this was about to change.

I took an early morning hike up the same trail, but saw no bears. I decided to take another trail that would lead me to the road. I still saw no bears. I finally reached a road and started hiking back. I was almost back to the start when I ran into Joseph Brady who was looking into the woods. There was the grizzly family about 30 yards away, slowly moving in the same direction as we were. We continued along the road to a parking area where they soon showed up.

We were blown away by what we saw next. The entire family group started rubbing on the creosote- soaked timbers set up as curbs (Photo 50). They were totally mesmerized by these man-made objects as we were totally mesmerized by their actions. It seemed like they were making love to these wooden objects. We watched them for about 20 minutes as they rubbed all over the large poles lying along the pavement. They then began to rub on an adjacent tree (Photo 51) until a man with a camera ran in front of us, towards the bears. The bear family did not panic, but with the mother leading, they quit rubbing, moved through the now vacated developed area, got on another trail, and disappeared to the west. Once again, the family, particularly the mother, exhibited incredible tolerance.

Three weeks later I would see them for the last time in 2010. It was early November and there was less than a handful of people in the area where we last saw the grizzlies. Shane "Mono" Connor and I had gone over for the day to see if we could find this fascinating family. Sure enough, when we got there, they were about 100 yards above the road eating kinnikinnick berries. We watched them for quite some time.

As they neared a rocky area, the mother moved towards

Photo 50

Photo 51

the road. The chubby cubs in their winter coats, followed (Photo 52). They crossed the road, made their way through some thick woods, and popped out in a grassy area. There, they spent some time grazing . Finally, they disappeared into thick cover next to a large lake. We wished them a successful hibernation and hoped we would see all four the next season. We would not be disappointed.

I was not able to visit the area until the later part of August 2011. I took a hike with Joseph early in the morning. As we were about half way to our destination, Joseph called my name. I looked back at him as he was pointing to the trail in front of me. To my surprise two yearling grizzlies were happily bouncing down the trail towards us. I had been making noise and looking on both sides of the trail in the heavy cover. Joseph was looking straight ahead and spotted

Photo 52

them first. The mother and other cub showed up. Joseph and I backed down the trail to a place where we could safely get off the trail and let the family pass. When we stopped, the grizzly family walked right by us on the trail then went up the side of the mountain, eating serviceberries as they climbed. After three hours they disappeared over a rocky ridge.

The next morning, we hiked the same trail without seeing the family. We sat down to take a break and glass the entire area. There, about 400 yards above us, was the mother grizzly and her yearlings eating huckleberries in a historically great patch. They were visible for about 10 minutes before they moved out of sight.

One week later, on August 30, I saw the mother grizzly about 100 yards above the trail in the same area. I looked around and saw one of the cubs. They were busily eating hucks and moving towards the trail. The mother and the one cub dropped onto the trail and started moving towards me. I still had not seen the other two cubs. It was now almost 10 a.m. and a lot of people were hiking up the trail. I started moving back down the trail as the mother grizzly and one cub approached (Photo 53). I soon met groups of people hiking up towards me and the bears. I informed them of what was happening. By now they could also see the mother and cub coming down the trail toward us.

I told them to remain calm and stay together. We started moving down the trail together in an orderly fashion, even though the two bears were not far behind. We needed to find an appropriate spot to get off the trail to let the bears by us, if they so desired. I now saw the other two cubs quickly descending the mountainside in order to catch up with their mother and sibling. There was no place to get off the trail because both sides were far too steep. We continued backing

Photo 53

up. Our group of hikers now numbered about twenty. Beyond us was another group of about twenty that I barely noticed, since my attention was on the bears coming down the trail towards us.

The two lagging sibling cubs finally caught up with the mother and other cub, at which time they appeared to celebrate their reunion (Photo 54). This did not slow them down and they continued down the trail towards us. At this time the other group of hikers started to panic. I could hear screaming and someone yelling "killer grizzlies!" My main attention was still on the bear family and the group of people I was with, none of whom panicked. We finally came to a small flat knoll where we could get off the trail. We did so and the mother grizzly and two of the cubs promptly went past us on the trail (Photo 55).

Photo 54

Photo 55

One of the cubs, however, left the trail and went around us on our other side. Here we were between a mother grizzly and her cub—a classically dangerous situation. Orange Sunshine showed no concern. It was at this point that the other group of people started running and scattering into the woods like a herd of cats. The bears paid no attention and as soon as they got around us, they started up the mountain into a patch of serviceberries where they ate their way out of sight.

We lingered for a bit and discussed what had happened. The people I was with were very thankful for what they had just witnessed. For most it was an experience of a lifetime. Many of them continued hiking. The group that was behind us was not seen again. Apparently, they ran down the trail and "informed" park personnel of the "killer grizzlies." A few of us slowly hiked down the trail, thinking that the family would make another appearance. Farther down the trail we sat down and took a break. During this time Joseph and some other friends had hiked up and met us.

A park bear ranger also showed up. While I was relating the events of the morning, the mother grizzly and her three cubs made another appearance. This time it was almost in exactly the same place as a year earlier. There was now another photographer and another bear ranger at that part of the trail (Photo 56). However, this time the bear family turned around and headed towards us and started eating serviceberries near the trail.

The second bear ranger apparently closed the trail behind him so no more people would hike up. Both rangers knew this bear family and knew that they were not "killer grizzlies." We all stood calmly in one area (except for the other Ranger and photographer who were on the other side of the bears) and watched them. One of the cubs started playing with a "closed

Photo 56

Photo 57

area" sign about 30 yards away and tore it down (Photo 57). The ranger with us said in a sarcastic voice, "bad bear!" Of course, we all laughed. The family slowly made it's way uphill and disappeared in thick brush. We continued down the trail. The rangers stayed for a bit then came down and reopened the trail. Once again, this amazing grizzly family displayed remarkable tolerance of all kinds of people and a myriad amount of human reactions. I would see this family one more time that year.

In early November I made one more trip to this special part of the park, hoping to see the bear family as I had the year before at this time. Joseph was there when I showed up. It did not take long to find them. They were in the same spot as the previous year, once again eating kinnikinnick berries right above the road (Photo 58).

After watching them for about an hour, it started to snow. The mother, as the year before, moved towards the road. The family group walked right down the road where they kind of wandered around in the heavy snowfall (Photo 59) and finally disappeared into the forest. After about 30 minutes, the sun came out and melted all of the snow. Two hours later the family showed up where we had first seen them that morning: above the road eating kinnikinnick. It would be the last time I ever saw all four of them together.

Over those two seasons this beautiful mother grizzly and her rambunctious cubs taught me an incredible amount. She showed me how intelligent and adaptable these animals really are. She was a great mother that cared for her offspring the best way she could in an area filled with both knowledgeable people and idiots. Her toleration was not caused by people, but was a survival tactic in order to take advantage of the incredible food sources existing amongst thousands of tourists.

Photo 58

Photo 59

She also used the presence of people for safety from the large males that avoid humans. She was successful. She kept all three cubs alive and very healthy through 2 full seasons.

YELLOWSTONE NATIONAL PARK, MAY 2019
815 and 3 cubs-of-the-year

Steve Merlino and I left his house about 5:30 am. It was a clear and cold morning. Our objective was to check out reports of recent sightings of grizzlies along some roads in Yellowstone. Hiking was out of the question due to the deep snow cover over much of the park. After carefully scouting out areas where we had seen grizzlies in previous years, we headed to an area where we had seen many grizzlies early in the year. However, when we came to the junction to turn, we decided to go straight to check out an area that was fairly close and a, now three-year-old, grizzly was seen the previous year with its mother. This mother was known as 815. Her home range included the area we were about to explore.

We came around a curve in the road near a small lake and some open areas and noticed a few vehicles parked in pullouts. We figured the three-year-old was out, but saw nothing. We approached some of the people that were out of their cars and trucks to get some information. We were told that 815 and three new cubs had been sighted right in that spot the night before—the first sighting of her that year. We were very excited. We were glad that we had not turned at the junction.

Three hours later we were beginning to question our decision. We were talking about leaving, to look for bears where we originally wanted to go earlier in the morning, when suddenly, to our amazement, the mother grizzly and her very small cubs (cubs-of-the-year: cubs born in the den that winter—also referred to as spring cubs) came out of a very thick stand of lodgepole pine. She approached an open area right by the road (Photo 60). Patience is certainly a virtue, as I am finally beginning to learn as I get older.

The three cubs were very wary of coming close to the road. Most of the time only one or two of the cubs would come near the road with the mother. The lightest one, wanted nothing to do with the, now growing, bear jam (Photo 61); showing its displeasure by bawling at the mother (Photo 62). The family group didn't move far. The mother and usually the one cub would move in and out of the forest as they took turns grazing on the new, tender grass, in the open, and taking short naps in the heavy cover. We left at about 7 p.m., vowing to return the next morning.

We arrived at the same spot at the same time as the previous day. As we came around the same curve, we were astonished

Photo 60

to see, not the bears, but a multitude of vehicles. Apparently, word of 815 and her new cubs spread like wildfire. Once again, we sat and waited. After 4 hours (this time), we started to talk about leaving. By this time the bear jam had grown to over 100 vehicles, even though no bears had been sighted yet. Before we left, we decided to walk down the road behind the scores of photographers. They already set up their tripods, even though they had no idea where the bears might pop up, if they did at all.

I soon ran into some very nice women along with some friends, who had also heard about the previous day's episode. I noticed that some of the ladies were peering intently into the woods. One of them said they saw some movement. They pointed out the area. Then something moving caught my eye. It was the cubs chasing each other far back in the thick stand of trees. These bears were now becoming active after,

Photo 61

Photo 62

what was probably, a long nap. I looked up and down the line of photographers and noticed nobody was paying attention because they couldn't see anything, and they seemed to be all talking to each other in small groups.

As the previous day, our patience paid off. The mother and her three cubs popped out, across the road, right in front of us (Photos 63 and 64). If I had my camera on a tripod, I would never have gotten these photos. The other photographers did not have room to reposition their tripods to get this angle, unless they were already right there. They were stuck where they originally set up. Mobility can be a distinct advantage. It can also help for getting out of the way if the bears move too close or if people start doing crazy things (which, much to our chagrin, we would see later that day). For this reason, I always carry bear spray in any road situation.

As the previous day, 815 and her cubs would move back and forth from the roadside into the forest. However, we could see a change in the cub's behavior. The two skittish cubs were now becoming more accustomed to the roadside situation. Unfortunately, because of this changing behavior, the bears were getting closer to the road on every return from their retreat in the woods (Photo 65). Thankfully, by this time park rangers were on the scene trying to control the crowds that were now, seemingly, everywhere. The rangers did as good a job as they could based on the number of people. Even then, people were still approaching the family group and parking illegally. After witnessing this "circus," we decided to leave. However, we still wanted to come back the next day.

Once again, we arrived at the area about the same time. In contrast to the previous mornings, however, there was hardly

Photo 63

Photo 64

anyone around and definitely no bears. We didn't quite understand what was going on. After waiting a little bit, we decided to continue down the road. We saw no further bear activity. We turned around and went back. When we arrived to where the bears had been the previous days, we were quite surprised to , first, see a few vehicles, and then the bear family on the other side of the road! We had only been gone about an hour. What happened?

We soon learned that the bears had crossed the road earlier in the morning and bedded down under a nearby boardwalk. They popped out right before we got back (Photo 66). I sent the next two hours videoing the cubs who were running all over a large open area. What a difference two days make!

During the two-hour period the number of vehicles grew from about a dozen to way over 100. It would eventually

Photo 65

grow into the largest bear jam I had ever seen. Any attempt to move was futile. There were rangers everywhere. The scene was becoming sad—not only for the bears, but to see the behavior of the people. We packed up and left. I would not come back. I spent the night at Steve's, where we discussed the last three days' activities. I had never seen such a rapid change in cub's behavior and dynamics of the roadside's scene. What we witnessed over those three days is one reason, but not the only one, that grizzlies become tolerant: they learn it from their mother.

There are, of course, other reasons. The other factor in this case, was the early availability of spring food. This particular area was one of the first to green up, largely due to the nearby thermal features. Avoidance of large male bears (as we had first seen in Denali), was not a big factor at this time of year,

Photo 66

since this was mating season. During this time males are more concerned with amorous activities instead of being away from people. Also, for family groups to avoid mature males, they would have to forgo the food source that was in this area, which in and of itself would present a serious problem. Soon, I would reconfirm what I believe is the main reason grizzlies become tolerant: an abundant food source.

GRAND TETON NATIONAL PARK, 2020, 2021 AND 2022

399 and 4 cubs

I never imagined that I could see larger bear jams than that occurred with 815 and her 3 cubs in Yellowstone in 2019. I was wrong. I, also, never imagined that Grizzly 399 in the Tetons, at age 24, would appear with 4 cubs-of-the-year in the spring of 2020. Her appearance with 4 new cubs blew everyone away, including veteran 399 watchers! Word spread fast. As a result, bear watchers and photographers started to descend on the park. When this family group (Photo 67) was spotted, from or near the road, the bear jams quickly formed and over the course of the season grew in number of participants.

399 is a prime example of a tolerant grizzly and good mother. She kept her head at all times while most of the people were losing theirs. She traveled extensively, showing and finding her brood various food sources. Because of her experience, she had an extensive knowledge of the ecosystem. She could disappear as fast as she appeared. I learned a lot from this amazing grizzly. She kept all 4 cubs into hibernation. After they denned up, speculation immediately focused on the spring and whether she would come out with all 4. I had seen grizzlies with 4 cubs-of-the-year before, but had never seen a family group with 4 yearlings. I was excited and apprehensive, 399 would be 25 years old.

Once again, to our delight, 399 did not disappoint. She came out on April 15, 2021 with her 4 yearling cubs! I did not see her until my trip in May. Within one hour of arriving, she and her cubs suddenly appeared from thick willows into a small open area (Photo 68). A very large bear jam quickly developed. After about an hour of grazing and digging biscuitroot, they disappeared as fast as they appeared. I would watch them over the next 4 days at various times and places as they traveled over a large area.

The last 2 days I observed them was probably the most dynamic. They moved along the shores of Jackson Lake (Photo 69) crossed the road and, once again, started grazing and digging biscuit root before movie to the south and

Photo 67

Photo 68

Photo 69

Photo 70

disappearing into thick forest. They would pop out briefly the rest of the day causing many bear jams.

The next day they started their way back to where I had first seen them. Of course, they started many bear jams. The last was probably the largest I had ever witnessed. They stopped in one small area right next to the road and, surprise, started grazing and digging biscuitroot (Photo 70). They then came down to the road and began heading north, weaving their way through the stopped vehicles (Photo 71). The people farther back in the line of vehicles probably never knew what all the "commotion" was about - a not uncommon occurrence. 399 reminded me of some of the other tolerant mother grizzlies I had seen over the years, especially 264 in Yellowstone and Orange Sunshine in Glacier.

In May of 2022 I was fortunate to see this family group for the last time. Once again 399 successfully appeared with all four cubs on April 16. The two-year-olds appeared healthy when I saw them on May 2 (Photo 72, 399 is second from the left). I saw them again on May 4 in almost the same place along Jackson Lake as Photo 69 in 2021. I was only able to capture the bears one by one because they were so spread out. This time 399 brought up the rear (Photo 73). She appeared to be slowing down as her cubs were getting more rambunctious. A week after I took this photo, she chased off the last of the cubs near the location of Photo 72. Hopefully, all of these cubs will live long and prosperous lives like their mother, who is now 26. She is a most remarkable bear.

Katmai National Park, September 2018, 2019, and 2021

Katmai National Park may be the ultimate place to observe

Photo 71

Photo 72

Photo 73

tolerant grizzlies. The grizzlies' behavior here reminds me a lot of the roadside bears in Yellowstone and Grand Teton National Parks and the grizzlies along or near the trails in Glacier. The main difference is the food source: salmon—lots of salmon, and the number of grizzlies. Sockeye salmon are the most numerous and have the longest run (Photo 74). There is a later silver salmon run in September, but the sockeye can still be running. This results in the bears having a long, abundant, and reliable food source. Like berries, though, some years are better than others.

The other thing about Katmai is that, in some areas, both large males, sub-adults, and family groups can all be present. This fact, in and of itself, seems to contradict one of the main reasons for bears being near people: to avoid the big boys. In Katmai the lay of the land allows all bears the room to safely

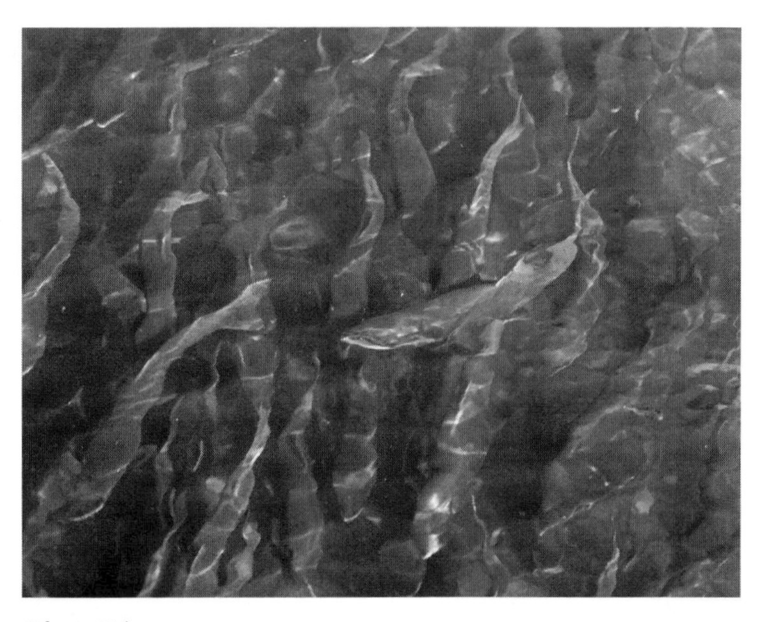

Photo 74

Photo 75

pursue the food source. The larger males and some large females take over the best fishing spots (Photos 75 and 76). The remaining areas are used by other grizzlies resulting, in most cases, lack of dangerous encounters between the bears themselves.

The advantage of observing tolerant bears is being able to experience behavior that would otherwise be difficult or impossible to see. Some of this behavior involves catching fish (Photo 77), nursing (Photo 78), play activity (Photo 79), lake fishing in high wind conditions (Photo 80), and even the activity of a mother bear with four cubs, which is rather rare (Photo 81).

Both bear watchers and fisherman come to Katmai. Some areas are more popular than others based on ease of access, fishing success, and facilities. In the area I visited in 2018 2019, and 2021, all three factors were present. In addition, ease of getting from point A to point B once on the ground, also existed. These factors meant that not only many bears were around, but there were also many people.

I was amazed to see so many large males packed into such a small area so close to people. On the other hand, the sub-adults and females with cubs were present in larger areas of the river bottom, along with many people. In both cases the bears basically ignored our presence. The result, as in Glacier and Yellowstone/Teton was the ability to observe behavior at close range, but with a higher number of bears.

Even though these bears were tolerant and were close, my safety protocol was no different than anywhere else I hike in grizzly country. I made noise and carried two cans of bear spray. As usual, most of the time I had one can out with the safety off. We would encounter grizzlies just about anywhere we hiked, including trails, beaches, roads (yes, they

Photo 76

Photo 77

Photo 78

Photo 79

Photo 80

Photo 81

do have a very limited road system in Katmai), and below the boardwalks. The latter did not present a problem, but we needed to be 50 yards from the bears, if possible, to avoid changing their behavior. I never noticed a change in behavior due to our actions. However, I did notice fisherman and photographers, in or near the river, have an effect on some behavior. These people were not on trails, but were usually involved in bushwhacking or wading. As in Glacier on busy trails or in Yellowstone/Teton along the roads, grizzlies can exhibit incredible tolerance if you are in a spot where your presence is expected.

About 2000, a few people postulated that that the grizzlies in Katmai had "acquired" a gene for tolerance. This "idea" was soon shattered in 2003 when Timothy Treadwell (who did not use bear spray) and his girlfriend were killed. When I was first in Katmai in 2018, some photographers told me I didn't need to carry bear spray. They said that the grizzlies in the area were "not like those in Yellowstone or Glacier." Obviously, I did not agree. From my added experience in 2019, I believe they are very similar in behavior (although they are larger) to those bears. Tolerance, as stated earlier, is nearly identical in areas of heavy human use.

I talked to rangers in Katmai both years. All rangers, bear techs, and interpreters, without exception, carry bear spray (Photo 82). Some have even had to use it. Many believe that sooner or later, a serious encounter will occur in the most popular portion of the park. In other words, it is not a matter of "if" but "when." Never, ever assume that a tolerant bear will always be so. There are too many things we know nothing about concerning bear behavior. Always respect bears and, for that matter, all things wild, including the animals, the infrastructure in these places,

Photo 82

Photo 83

Photo 84

Photo 85

and the ecosystem in general. The examples in this chapter reinforce this idea.

More bears (and other wildlife) will exhibit tolerant behavior as human population and activity increase. This will lead to more infrastructure that will be needed to accommodate the increased visitation. This will, in turn, lead to more visitation and activity. For example, in the most popular area in Katmai, a new bridge and viewing platforms were built between 2018 and 2019 (Photo 84). The old bridge (Photo 83) was much closer to the water. The new bridge, because it was much higher, enabled the bears to move more freely, while at the same time allowing more people to view the grizzlies at a closer distance (Photo 85).

We did not go to Katmai in 2020 because of Covid and the resulting travel restrictions. We were able to go in 2021 and observed that the bears were just as (or even more) "comfortable" with the new bridge (Photo 86). The downside is that these new structures will also draw more people to the area. This in turn will put more people close to the bears and more stress on the new and older infrastructure. This results in a, seemingly, endless cycle that will ultimately result in over-stressing the entire ecosystem. Tolerant bears are not the problem—people are. The only solution, I believe, is in some kind of permit system. In other words, limit the number of people that can access these vulnerable areas. This not only applies to Katmai, but Glacier and Yellowstone/Teton, too.

As more people visit all of these areas, the chances of somebody doing something stupid increases dramatically. Tolerant behavior on the part of any wildlife should not be interpreted as being tame. Petting wildlife is not unheard of. In Yellowstone I have witnessed people petting bison (Photo

87). Repeating such activity with a seemingly tolerant grizzly, let alone a bison, is not advised.

Another problem for many of these grizzlies, and for that matter all grizzlies, is the exposure to human sources such as garbage, animal feed, and bee hives. This last year (2021), in the Tetons and Glacier, at least 7 different grizzlies were euthanized due to exposure to garbage. 399 and her cubs were also at risk in the Jackson area. As a result 2 of her cubs were captured and radio-collared to help wildlife officials keep track of the family group. All of this could have been easily avoided if people took some simple steps such as securing their garbage and animal feed in a safe place. Chicken coops and bee hives, for example, can be secured with rather inexpensive electric fences. Recently, in the Jackson area, action was taken to confront and remedy some of these situations. Bear-proof garbage containers will

Photo 86

Photo 87

be required. In order to help, some non-profit organizations are providing resources to make sure everyone can comply. Hopefully, this and similar actions, including education, will solve some of these problems that are mostly caused by the increase in visitation and ever expanding population growth throughout the grizzlies' range.

CHAPTER ELEVEN

DEADLY ENCOUNTERS

Yellowstone National Park, August 2015

On August 7, 2015 a hiker was found dead in the Lake area of Yellowstone National Park. A few days later it was determined that a grizzly killed and partially consumed the 63-year-old man, and the suspected bear was a female with two cubs-of-the-year. Of course, the media coverage, both traditional and social, was intense. Unfortunately, this single event tragically reinforced most of the discussions and recommendations in the preceding chapters.

The hiker was reported missing on the morning of August 7 when he did not report for work at the Lake Urgent Care Clinic. A search discovered his body about three hours later near the Elephant Back Loop Trail, an area he was known to hike. The body was found about a mile from the trailhead and about one-third of a mile off the trail.

A recovery team discovered that the body was partially consumed and was covered with dirt, leaves, and sticks, as is typical of a carcass being utilized by a grizzly. Traps were set up and all the suspect grizzlies, the adult female and two cubs-of-the-year, were captured. DNA analysis proved that the captured female was the bear that killed the hiker. She was euthanized and the cubs were sent to a zoo in Toledo, Ohio.

The hiker was described by friends and associates as an

experienced hiker. He had worked in Yellowstone for five summers. Yet on the fatal hike, he was hiking alone, he was bushwhacking off trail, and he was not carrying bear spray. Was he making noise? We will never know. Nor will we ever know the exact circumstances of the encounter. Did he surprise the bears at close range?

Public reaction to the incident was intensified by the fact that three grizzlies were removed from the ecosystem, even though they may have been reacting in a totally natural manner, and because one of the bears was a cub-bearing female valuable to the threatened population.

There is no law that mandates hiking in a responsible and safe manner in grizzly country. There is no law that requires making noise or carrying bear spray. If someone wants to increase the risk of a negative encounter, that is apparently his or her right. However, jeopardizing the lives of magnificent animals in order to express some personal hiking philosophy does not sit well with many people, especially those that have a passion for the continued existence of grizzlies.

The public outcry over the fate of the bears increased dramatically when word spread that the mother bear was "Blaze," a bear well known to photographers and bear watchers (Photos 88 taken 2004, 89 taken in 2011, 90 taken in 2014). However, no one was able to positively identify the bear as Blaze (many Yellowstone grizzlies have a similar blaze marking behind the shoulder), and there were known to be at least four mother grizzlies with cubs-of-the-year in the Lake area, including (supposedly) Blaze. Finally, in early 2016, an analysis of the teeth of the euthanized female proved she was 11 to 13 years old, while the "Blaze" that I and others knew was at least 20 years old. So, Blaze did not kill the hiker, and Blaze was not killed by park authorities. Will we ever

Photo 88

Photo 89

Photo 90

see Blaze again? She was getting old for a grizzly. As of the writing of this book, if she was still alive, she would be at least 26 years old. Other grizzlies have lived longer. Let's hope Blaze does too.

Identification of individual bears throughout a single season and from year to year through behavior, areas utilized, and body structure and other physical characteristics is highly problematical.

Throughout this book I present many photos of certain grizzlies that I refer to by specific names. This implies that I know for sure which bears these are. In actuality, unless the particular grizzly was, for example, radio collared or has a distinctive marking (like Otis in Katmai with the distinctive 7 on his shoulder—see Photo 91) I am just making an educated guess based on prior observations. Of course, in most cases I

Photo 91

was "pretty sure" of the bear I observed, or I would not have used a name.

However, even if I know a grizzly well (a rather questionable assumption), my hiking precautions are based on the fact that ***what we perceive as a safe situation may not be what the bear perceives.*** Bears make up their own minds, and encounters can turn ugly very fast. As mentioned earlier, never assume a "tolerant" bear will always be tolerant. Conditions and circumstances change. You must always be careful, watchful, and prepare to use bear spray when in grizzly country. The next encounter reinforces this idea.

Teton Wilderness, Wyoming, September 2018

On September 13 a guide from Jackson, Wyoming and his client from Florida were elk hunting (with horses) in the

Teton Wilderness northeast of Jackson. The client shot an elk with a crossbow and wounded it. The guide and client searched for the elk, without success. They decided to come back the next day to continue their efforts, which they did.

At about 1 p.m. on September 14 they found the body of the elk. The guide started to field dress the elk. After a short time, they heard rocks falling down a nearby steep slope. This would be the beginning of a rather quick series of events. The aforementioned and what follows is based on an article, which itself is based on an investigative report from the Wyoming Game and Fish Department, published by the *Jackson Hole News and Guide* on January 30, 2019.

According to the client, "he looked up and saw two grizzly bears running full speed directly toward them." The guides first reaction was "waving his arms and yelling" in the moment before contact with the bear. It was a mother and yearling cub. The mother was the aggressor. The guide had bear spray in a holster on his left hip, but failed to use it at that time. The client had bear spray, but it was left in his pack because it had "become too cumbersome carrying it on the horse." I do not understand this. I carried bear spray on my hip for years whenever I rode my horse, without any problems whatsoever. In any event, the result, in this case, was that the guide was severely mauled and died near the scene.

What happened next is rather unclear. The client survived, but apparently gave conflicting statements to the investigating authorities. Because of this, and other factors, the report based its' findings on the evidence at the scene.

I will not go to every detail, but want to emphasize a few things:

(1) The guide was ultimately able to spray the attacking grizzly with his bear spray.

(2) The report stated that "Evidence suggests that when [the guide] deployed the bear spray, it stopped the aggression. However, this appears to be after the fatal injuries were inflicted." The evidence also indicated that after he managed to end the attack with a "blast of bear spray," he was able to stagger about 50 yards before succumbing to his injuries which included massive blood loss.

(3) A Wyoming Game and Fish official indicated that this grizzly attack was aberrant behavior.

As to item (1), this fact has been used by many opponents and/or skeptics of bear spray to downplay or even refute the effectiveness of this defensive tool. I could not disagree more! Their arguments totally ignore the evidence presented in item (2): that the spray was effective, but was used only after the fatal injuries were inflicted. The effectiveness of any weapon or tool could be refuted if such evidence was ignored.

I also believe that instead of waving his arms and yelling, if the guide used that time to pull his bear spray out of his holster and deploy it, the situation might have been far different. I, obviously, was not there and am in no position to second guess. However, I always emphasize that time is of the essence in utilizing bear spray effectively. This may be one example of that philosophy.

As to item (3), I definitely do not agree that this attack indicated aberrant behavior. Such behavior may be uncommon, but it has happened before: in 1995 in an area of British Columbia, about 200 miles north of where I live. It happened again in 2001 near Ovando, Montana, about 100 miles south of my residence. I read about both attacks at the time they occurred and remember them well. When I heard of this specific incident I was not surprised.

A recurrent theme in every grizzly attack, whether involving a fatality or injury, is that everyone is slightly different and evidence in every situation indicates that the people involved were not, in some way, following proper safety protocol. It should be noted that in this case, as in many other fatal cases (including the first discussed case), the involved bears were either killed or removed from the ecosystem by officials.

Lastly, many people use events as these as a reason why grizzlies should be hunted. The main argument is that bears will learn to run from people if hunted. In backcountry areas where I have spent considerable time, bears will almost always run from humans (if you don't surprise them at close range). This, I believe, can be attributed to the lack of human activity in these remote regions. All of these areas do not allow hunting of grizzlies. I see no reason why hunting in these areas would affect this outcome. In addition, no one has ever been able to tell me how a dead bear learns anything.

I believe deadly bear encounters—for the person and eventually the bear—are too common in an era when technology (bear spray) and common sense (making noise) should make these incidents extremely rare, if they occur at all. I believe it is incumbent on all of us that have a passion for the great bear to set a good example by carrying bear spray and making noise when we hike and recreate in grizzly country. We should also educate people on why our actions are important for the continued viability and survival of grizzlies, so that future generations can partake of the awe and wonder that we have had the good fortune to experience.

CHAPTER TWELVE

EDUCATION

How can more people hike safely in grizzly country? How do more people understand grizzly behavior and the important things the bear needs to survive? How do more people appreciate what grizzly country represents to the survival of wild animals and the health of the ecosystem in general? When do we realize that the principles we apply to tolerate the presence of the grizzly can be used to prevent the loss of everything wild?

Education must be the foundation of providing the answers. With gaining knowledge, we can begin to understand the results of our actions. We our educated in two ways: learning from other people and learning through our own experiences. Hopefully, this book can provide some of the necessary information to provide answers to the above questions.

Over the last 20 years I have sought to educate people on almost everything I have come to learn about grizzly bears. Almost everything I teach is based on my own experiences. My endeavors in this area have been meant to ensure that future generations are able to have the same opportunities I have had to experience observing grizzlies and their behavior in the wild areas that still exist. The best two examples of education on grizzlies that people can obtain in our National Parks are represented by the programs in Glacier National Park and Katmai National Park. I cannot think of any other programs that are so different in nature.

Glacier National Park Grizzly Bear Education

In Glacier, the educational opportunities are quite limited. This is rather surprising considering the number of visitors, bears, and close encounters. It is also remarkable in light of that fact that Glacier has experienced more fatalities from grizzly encounters than any other park. The only mandatory grizzly education offered is when one obtains a permit to camp in the backcountry. It is part of a short video that includes information on proper food storage, making noise, and what to do if a grizzly is encountered. The video only needs to be viewed by one person in each party.

All other education offered is rather limited, and none of which is provided in any detail. There is a park newspaper along with a small yellow pamphlet that is handed out at all entrance stations, if the visitor decides to accept the material. The newspaper has one page on safety in grizzly country. The yellow pamphlet also discusses safety in bear country. Visitor centers provide short videos on bear safety and "campfire talks" at select frontcountry campgrounds also provide such information on selected evenings. There are also small signs at most trailheads in small print that discusses safety. The best discussion of grizzlies and safety is provided on a rather large two-sided display at a pullout before visitors reach one of the entrance stations on the east side of the park. I rarely see anyone at this display. The result is that only a very small percentage of the 3 million visitors to Glacier obtain any valid bear safety education. However, what bear education is provided, carrying bear spray is encouraged.

Most people I observe and talk to on the trails in Glacier have no idea, whatsoever, of the significance of their actions and their impact on the ecosystem. About one-third to one-half of hiking groups have bear spray, although this represents an improvement over the past. Of the people that do carry bear spray, I have no idea if they know how to use it. People believe that garbage dumpsters are bear proof. They are not! (see Photo 92) Also, some of the smaller garbage cans can even overflow (see Photo 93).

Photo 92

Photo 93

The lack of proper education and the stress on facilities provides an unrealistic view of safety expectations. There also appears to be an attitude of complacency on the part of both visitors and the park itself. The last fatality from a grizzly encounter occurred in 1998. I am concerned that the attitudes and precautions displayed in Glacier and surrounding areas will result in undesired outcomes in the near future. Hopefully, I am wrong.

Katmai National Park Bear Education

My first visit to Katmai was in 2018. It was to the most popular area—the Brooks River location. I was pleasantly surprised, not only because of the presence and behavior of the grizzlies, but also due to the incredible emphasis on bear safety education. Everyone that visits Brooks must attend "Bear School." It is mandatory before anyone can hike, fish, or camp in the area. Classes are provided as needed. Most classes are presented at the visitor center. During the busy times of the season, a small auditorium, located in a nearby separate building may be used, in addition. During 2019 over 14,000 people attended these classes.

The class consists of a well-produced video. Afterwards, an overview of the video and a discussion of the surrounding area is provided. A question-and-answer period is the provided. The entire presentation takes 20-25 minutes, at the end of which small pins attesting to the fact that you attended are handed out. The class puts emphasis on basically five safety and awareness factors:

(1) How close you are allowed to get to bears—50 yards.
(2) Make noise while hiking or wading in the area.
(3) What to do if you encounter a bear at close range (which happens quite often)

- *never* run
- do not yell
- talk softly to the bear(s)
- if the bear approaches, find a place to safely move off the trail or out of its direction of travel
- hike in groups, if possible
- food and gear storage protocol

(4) fishing protocol
(5) boardwalk and platform viewing protocol

One thing I definitely noticed was that there was absolutely no mention of bear spray. After some thought, I realized the reason, which I confirmed with park staff. If everyone carried bear spray, bears would be getting sprayed left and right. Many people who are not properly trained in bear spray usage and bear behavior would freak out when encountering a bear at close range. These tolerant grizzlies can and are encountered at 30 feet or less on the trails, beaches, river, by the campground, by any buildings—basically anywhere in the area. I noticed that, as in Glacier one-third to one-half of the visitors carry bear spray. Many times, as anywhere in grizzly country, I had my bear spray out. I never needed to spray a bear, but did get into some questionable situations (see Photos 94, 95). I did learn that some rangers have had to spray grizzlies during their time at Brooks.

I would say that bear education works fairly well, considering the number of bears in close proximity to people at Brooks. However, I still saw people do stupid things (e.g., approaching bears way too close), as if they didn't learn anything at Bear School. The main causes are: (1) a lot of "daytrippers," i.e., people who only visit for one day and are not really able to observe the bears and the habitat for any

Photo 94

Photo 95

length of time; and (2) lack of enforcement of the rules laid out in class. For the most part, though, the vast majority of visitors follow the rules.

Another tool that is provided at Katmai is webcams that show grizzlies behavior throughout the Brooks River area. They can be viewed online by people all over the world. As a result, many people have the opportunity to view many different bears and their behavior. Some of us consider this a double edge sword. It is definitely educational, but also draws attention to a very fragile area that is becoming visited more and more because of this increased "publicity."

An offshoot of this program is the annual "fattest bear contest." Viewers vote online and at the end of the season the results are announced. In 2019 the semi-finalists were 747 (Photo 96), a large male and Holly, a very large female (Photo 97). Using advanced 3D scanning equipment, which we witnessed during our stay, it was determined that 747 weighed in at 1400 pounds and Holly at 700 pounds. Even though 747 was much bigger, Holly won the "award." I believe the photos accurately back up the final vote. This contest is, in my opinion, rather frivolous, but it promotes people's interest in grizzlies.

The main difference between Glacier and Katmai in regard to education can be attributed to the difference in the number of visitors to each park. As mentioned earlier, Glacier receives 3 million visitors or more a year. Katmai may receive at most 30,000-35000 visitors per year and about half of these are at Brooks. The maximum number of visitors that can stay overnight at Brooks are 120. Add in day visitors (daytrippers) and you are looking at 250-350 max per day. It makes it possible, logistically, to provide mandatory education. Glacier, on the other hand, has as many visitors, or more,

Photo 96

Photo 97

on busy days as all of Katmai has in a single year. There is no realistic way Glacier could mandate bear safety education, unless it was part of a day hiking by permit only program on certain trails. The mandatory education would then be part of obtaining such permit. This would also mean that the number of people hiking these certain trails would be subject to a daily maximum. Some limits have been implemented at Brooks, especially as it affects the river bottom area (Photo 98), due to the increasing number of day visitors.

No matter what solutions are devised in either park, increased visitation and the associated burden on infrastructure and wildlife will drive the discussion. The same debate is also appropriate for Yellowstone and Grand Teton National Parks due to the increase in human activity.

Photo 98

CONCLUSION

I have experienced and learned quite a bit since I saw my first grizzlies more than 37 years ago. The one thing that never ceases to amaze me is the more I learn, the more I realize how much I don't know. I can no longer deal in absolutes. Every time I think I have figured out the ways of the great bear, I observe something that I can't explain. For example, many times I have thought I have learned a particular area well enough to predict the presence of grizzlies, only to find no grizzlies when I thought they should be there. There are just too many variables, especially in an era of climate change.

The fate of the grizzly is at a crossroads. Because of our technological advancements we can fragment and destroy the bear population and habitat more rapidly than we can accurately judge the ramifications of our actions. Since I began my endeavors to observe grizzlies more than 37 years ago, the population of the United States has increased from 238 million people to more than 330 million. At the same time the population of grizzlies in the Lower 48 has also increased, due mainly to the Endangered Species Act, but by less than 1000. The resources needed to save the great bear for future generations is insignificant compared to the resources our increasing population utilizes, for example, to travel to grizzly country. Our national parks are being overwhelmed and thereby the core home for most of a grizzly population (in the lower 48) once estimated to be 100,000, is being quickly eroded. Food sources are still available throughout the grizzly's original range, but because of the sheer number of people intolerant of or ignorant of this majestic animal, the grizzly's future is not bright.

People who hike and/or recreate in grizzly country can help the future of the great bear. Just by using two basic safety protocols we can help reduce one of the most significant causes of the death or removal of grizzlies: unnecessary human caused encounters. Making noise and carrying bear spray will not only cut down on human injuries and death, but they will help reduce negative impacts on grizzly populations. The grizzly is important not just because it represents what is truly wild, but because these animals can teach us so much. It is hard for me to understand how an animal with such a vicious reputation and one that we push and persecute incessantly, can be so tolerant. Their intelligence, adaptability, and beauty, I think, are unrivaled in the animal kingdom.

In college I took Economics 101. The textbook was written by Nobel Prize winner Paul Samuelson. I will never forget his discussion of the value of things. He asked, "what is the value of clean air" and "what is the value of clean water?" I had never thought about economics in that context. At that time, these most essential resources were free. Most people had never even thought about assigning a value, let alone a dollar amount to their "worth."

What is a grizzly worth? (Photo 99) I believe they, as with clean air and water, are priceless. Unfortunately, many people would disagree. It is up to us, those who love the wild and the grizzly, to educate and set an example, so that our grandchildren and their grandchildren can appreciate and understand the incredible gift that all of us have been given.

Photo 99

ABOUT THE AUTHOR

After receiving his B.A. degree in mathematics from the University of Minnesota and a J.D. degree from William Mitchell College of Law, Tim Rubbert went to work in the insurance industry where he eventually became disillusioned with the corporate lifestyle. In 1989 he completed the PROBE secondary education program at the University of Colorado. Since 1985 he has devoted his life to the study, observation, and photography of grizzly bears. Tim has hiked various areas from Grand Teton National Park to Denali. He has hiked every trail in Glacier National Park and most of the trails in the Whitefish Range and the northern portion of the Great Bear Wilderness in Montana. He has also hiked extensively in the Greater Yellowstone Ecosystem. In the last 37 years, Tim has hiked more than 50,000 miles and experienced more than 3,000 grizzly sightings.

During his extensive travels, Tim has made a point of:

- Concentrating on backcountry observation to learn as much about grizzlies as possible with a minimum of intrusion.
- Focusing mainly on the Northern Continental Divide Ecosystem (NCDE).
- Documenting numerous backcountry encounters with grizzlies.
- Learning and teaching others about the proper use of bear spray, which he has had to use twice.
- Performing volunteer work with the National Biological Survey, observing grizzly bears in Denali National Park in 1994.

Tim has conducted educational slide presentations on

grizzlies in Alaska, British Columbia, Idaho, Wyoming, Minnesota, and Montana. He has conducted educational hikes on Big Mountain near Whitefish, Montana and has archived an extensive collection of grizzly bear, other wildlife, and scenic photos. He has also instructed classes at Flathead Valley Community College in Kalispell, Montana, on grizzly habitat and behavior. Tim lives with his wife, Suzi, in grizzly country in northwest Montana.